PESOS

PESOS

THE RISE AND FALL
OF A BORDER FAMILY

PIETRO LA GRECA JR.
WITH REBECCA PALEY

Published by Little A, New York

www.apub.com

Amazon, the Amazon logo, and Little A are trademarks of Amazon.com, Inc., or its
affiliates.

ISBN-13: 9781542033466 (hardcover)
ISBN-10: 1542033462 (hardcover)

ISBN-13: 9781542033442 (paperback)
ISBN-10: 1542033446 (paperback)

Cover design by Faceout Studio, Lindy Martin

Printed in the United States of America

First edition

AUTHOR'S NOTE: The events in this book, which come from conversations with
my father, other family members, and friends, have been portrayed to the best of
my memory. Some names and identifying details have been changed to protect the
people involved.

To my wife, Michelle, and daughter, Gabriella, you both are the inspirational lantern of my life. Make sure that every day you continue to build your world.

PROLOGUE

I was on the couch at home, watching football—the Chargers were in the playoffs in January 2014—when the phone rang. It was my lawyer.

"Your dad had a fall. He's at Scripps Memorial," he said, referring to the La Jolla hospital only six miles from my apartment.

"Frank, who'd you hear this from?"

My first thought was that my father had called Frank himself and was bluffing. I wouldn't have put it past him. He was, after all, a con man. He'd been one his whole life. As a young man, he'd sweet-talked his way from Napoli to San Diego on a rich woman's yacht and into a marriage with the daughter of one of Tijuana's most prominent families. From there, he'd gone on to make millions illegally washing money by turning pesos into dollars for the most important politicians, businessmen, and celebrities in Mexico. Then, when his legendary temper got the best of him, he'd eventually lost those millions and everything else my family owned.

Well, not everything.

Frank told me he'd heard the news from Esquerro, the lawyer who represented corrupt cops in Tijuana and whom my father had hired to represent him in his legal battle against me. The battle was for the last remaining piece of what had once been a vast family empire that had stretched from an opulent mansion in Coronado—a yacht bobbing in the water right outside the front lawn—all the way to a ranch that stretched across two hundred acres of Rosarito, from the rugged desert mountains to the white-sand beaches. Halfway between these two properties, smack on the world's busiest border in San Ysidro, stood my maternal grandfather's customs brokerage building. The building was my inheritance, and my father was trying to sell it out from under me. His betrayal had been, for me, the last straw in a long string of broken promises and lies.

"Okay, great. My father is in the hospital. I don't care anymore."

The last time I talked to my father in person had been a few months earlier when he asked to meet me at California Pizza Kitchen. Over arugula salad with breaded chicken (his favorite dish because it reminded him of chicken Milanese), he'd brandished a piece of paper he wanted me to sign. But he had given me only the signature page of the document. He still thought of me as a naive little boy he could manipulate.

"What is this?" I asked him.

"Don't worry about it," he said. "Just fucking sign it."

"I can't sign it without seeing it."

"You'll do what I tell you!"

True to form, my dad began yelling at the top of his lungs. Other people in the restaurant glanced over at us nervously. I didn't care. Not one of his barrage of verbal punches landed. He could scream all he wanted. I'd already gotten wind that my father was trying to illegally sell my grandfather's building without letting me know, and I wasn't going to sign so much as a cocktail napkin for him.

Now, the news that my dad was in the hospital didn't faze me. I figured the worst that had happened was a mild heart attack or ministroke, and he was probably recuperating by now. He'd had high blood pressure and a weak heart for as long as I could remember. I knew my dad better than anyone else. This was a man who had opened dozens of bank accounts in my name when I was in middle school, unbeknownst to me, as part of one of the biggest money-laundering schemes in Mexican history. He bluffed when he needed to. He would use anything to get the upper hand in our battle over my building, even a son's sympathy for a father who suffered from a heart condition.

But he was barking up the wrong tree. The old man was a survivor. At eighty-three years old, he was still pretending to be the man who once went toe-to-toe with the president of Mexico. My father—El Italiano, as he was known even now—wore his Brioni silk shirts and Canali slacks everywhere, even to Home Depot. The man didn't know how to go casual. A vain man, he persisted in slicking back his full head of hair, which he'd been dyeing black since he got his first grays at fifty.

His care about appearances extended beyond his clothes and hair. Despite the fact that he didn't have the money to justify the extravagant fleet of cars, he'd kept his beloved Mercedes and Bentleys long after he couldn't drive anymore. (He failed the eye exam at the DMV when he went to renew his driver's license because he couldn't see, and he was too proud to wear glasses.)

He also ate dinner at La Jolla's most popular and expensive restaurants, and he tipped C-notes at his favorite spots, Eddie V's and Manhattan, like they were hard candies from an old man's pocket. Even though he was an octogenarian, he still wanted to live like a baller. That life included spending money on Judy, the heavily made-up girlfriend half his age whom he'd met at his condo, where she worked as a leasing agent in the building's rental office.

He'd been burning through the considerable amount of rent my grandfather's building brought in every month. And now, my dad—who for my whole life had always seemed to need more money—wanted to sell the property for a big payday. There was no way I was going to let him do that. It wasn't just about the money. I had a great job working in corporate America. But the customs building was the last tie to my mother's family and the dynasty they had once owned. The way I saw it, one of us was going down in this battle, and it wasn't going to be me.

As the conversation with my lawyer continued, however, I learned that my dad's condition in the hospital was not, in fact, part of some ruse. He'd had a freak fall exiting an SUV in front of his condo in Del Mar and severed almost every ligament around his neck. EMTs had rushed him to the hospital, where he underwent emergency surgery. He was currently in the ICU, and his prognosis was unclear.

"What do you want to do?" my lawyer asked.

"I don't know what I can do."

I didn't want to go to the hospital to see him, even if he was at death's door.

In subsequent days, family friends, who had a soft spot in their hearts for my dad, thought I was the coldest son of a bitch on the planet. What they didn't know was that a week before his fall, he had left me a threatening voice mail. Despite having spent most of his life in Baja California and neighboring San Diego, he still spoke in broken Spanish with a thick Italian accent.

"You cross that border into Mexico," he'd said in that thick accent, "and I will put you in your tomb."

Most people would have a hard time taking that threat from father to son literally. But when it came to Pietro La Greca, you never knew exactly where you stood.

CHAPTER 1

Burn It Down

Never ask a man how he made his first million dollars," my dad used to say.

Although he loved to talk about how he'd made *his* first million any chance he got. On Friday nights when I was a kid, he could be found at Matteottis, an old-school Italian restaurant in downtown Tijuana where he and his cronies hung out: talking, eating, drinking, and flirting with anyone in a skirt until two or three in the morning. Even after he moved our family to San Diego, Matteottis was his spot. Throughout my childhood, the restaurant—which even catered my baptism—kept the corner table reserved for my dad. That's where he told and retold the story of how young Pietro La Greca had left his small town outside Naples, found adventure on the high seas, and arrived in America to seek—and find—his fortune. I heard the story over and over and over again, which is why I can tell it now with such ease.

As a teenager, my father had watched American tanks roll through his hometown of Caserta, had seen the soldiers handing out SPAM and hot dogs to its residents. During World War II, Italy had joined Germany and Japan in fighting against the Allies, led by the United States, the UK, and the Soviet Union. When the Allies won the war in 1945, Italians had poured out of their homes onto the streets, full of gratitude for the Americans who'd rescued them from fascism and Mussolini's dictatorship. Ever since that day, my father had thought of the United States as the international savior. In his old age, he would still indulge his taste buds on a weekly basis with SPAM for breakfast and a fast-food cheeseburger from In-N-Out. As much as he loved his native Italy, until his dying day, he loved the US even more.

My dad came from a wealthy family on his mother's side that owned Chirico Molini e Pastificio, their eponymous pasta factory. His family and the employees of the pasta factory had survived the Allied bombings of World War II by taking shelter in the cellars of the factory. Despite his family's prominent standing in the community, however, my father's dream was always to come to America.

One day, as a young man, he got his chance. During a weekend in Rome with friends, he met an older American woman, who invited the handsome and charming Italian back to her place. He soon learned that her "place" was a yacht docked at one of the exclusive marinas that were located on the outskirts of the ancient city. Although his family members were big shots in his small town, their lifestyle was nothing compared to this. My father saw servants running to attend to the American woman's every wish. A bottle of chilled champagne appeared on the massive yacht's immaculate deck for the two of them to enjoy. This was his first taste of big-time wealth; he was hooked.

My father had always had a big ego. Even as a little kid, he'd reportedly paraded through the piazza like he owned the place. But he was plagued by insecurity that led him to constantly compare himself with others. Once he'd pulled out the measuring stick and discovered that someone else had more of something than he did, what he had was no longer good enough. This was always the case for him, and it was a problem that haunted him his entire life. When he wanted more of something, he pursued it without caring a bit about the havoc he left behind. As soon as he was introduced to the luxury on display aboard the American woman's yacht, running a pasta factory lost all its appeal. The family business that had once seemed so lucrative now struck him as peasants' work.

The next morning, when he awoke on the yacht, my father was alarmed to find a man in the cabin and to learn that he was none other than the woman's husband.

"I would like to have a conversation with you," the man said.

Instead of threatening my father, however, the woman's husband propositioned him. Would the young man like to be first mate on the private yacht as it returned to San Diego, where the couple lived? My dad's chief duty would be to keep the wealthy man's wife company while she was on the boat, since the much older man was no longer physically able to have sex. My dad happily agreed to come on board.

When he told his family that he had gotten a job as the manager of a rich American's yacht and was setting sail for the US, he conveniently left out his most important responsibility—the part about him having to satisfy the sexual needs of the man's wife. Appearing like a kept man would have been a huge embarrassment to him and brought shame to his family, who followed the old-world ways of Caserta.

Years later, however, in the gunslinging town of Tijuana—a lawless place where border-hopping Americans came to party and machismo was the norm—my father wore like a badge of honor the story of bedding a gorgeous, wealthy woman for pay. If I heard that story once from my dad, I heard it a hundred times. It didn't matter to him that people often pointed out that getting paid to have sex had made him a gigolo. As far as he was concerned, the story reinforced his reputation as a lover. It also served as part of the larger-than-life mythology that pervaded nearly every aspect of his history and made me—and many others— question constantly whether what Jefe was saying was real or bullshit. (From an early age, I called my dad *Jefe* because he bossed me around so much; I instinctively referred to him the way his employees did.)

The line between real and made up was always blurred when it came to my dad, because he always thought he was telling the truth. It helped that he believed his own lies. As he would teach me later: "Find the truth and get as close to it as you can, then embellish—or edit." Jefe immersed himself in his own mythology, turning up the volume on certain details when he needed to exaggerate or hushing up when he didn't want people to know certain facts. He knew that if one tells a story enough—even if it isn't completely true—then that story begins to feel like a memory, like it really happened.

Despite the healthy skepticism I grew to have regarding my father's history, there were plenty of times when stories I questioned were later validated. For example, he once told me that his father had tied him to a tree when he was a boy, as punishment for pushing his youngest sister in the back and yelling at her. Jefe's father had left him there for the entire night! My father had a terrible temper of his own, but in my mind, not even he would do something as cruel as that. I assumed the anecdote was another exaggeration intended to make him look like a tough guy. Later, however, on a family trip I took with my parents to Caserta when I was in high school, my surviving aunts confirmed the story and clarified it.

"He didn't just get tied up once," one of them said. "It was many times."

This was not the only one of my father's larger-than-life tales to get verified during my high school years. Another had to do with a period of his life he was very proud of: his brief car-racing career back in Italy.

Jefe had started racing cars for Ferrari in his early twenties. When he told me this, I believed—especially after he showed me his official racing license—that he might have, indeed, raced some cars. But I thought the story about his career-ending crash, in which his racing partner had been burned alive, was surely one of his creative embellishments. That is, until the day I accompanied him to the dentist.

My father had a mouthful of fake teeth, which he claimed he'd gotten as a result of his near-death crash during the Mille Miglia, a famous three-day, thousand-mile race that ran from Brescia to Rome and back. During the race, drivers and their co-drivers sped through countrysides, cities, and medieval towns, along narrow Italian roads that were lined with fans. The race was banned for decades in 1957, after a gruesome accident killed not only a car's driver and co-driver but also a number of spectators lining the road. All in all, more than fifty drivers died in the competition before the ban took effect.

When the dentist asked how it came about that he'd had all his teeth removed and replaced as a young man, my dad replied that while racing for Ferrari in the Mille Miglia, he and his partner had crashed. His partner, who had used his seat belt, remained in the car and burned to death. My dad, who hadn't worn a seat belt, was ejected and survived. But a small piece of metal had lodged into the flesh under his jaw and shattered all his teeth. The dentist, who turned out to be a racing enthusiast, knew the whole history of the race. "I've read about your race!" he said excitedly. I was shocked at the dentist's confirmation of my dad's exploits—and my dad was thrilled. (In fact, he remained loyal to the same dentist for many years, until the man retired.)

One story I had no trouble believing was the tale of how my father got his Ferrari. That story completely jibed with my perception of the man who would stop at nothing to get his way. As the story went, Dad had wanted to become a race-car driver. This was, in the eyes of his family, completely out of the question. All four of his older brothers had been killed in the Italo-Ethiopian War. This meant he was the only male left to take over the family pasta business.

However, my father wasn't just the only remaining son; he was also the second to youngest of ten siblings. His older sisters doted on him, treating him like a king and giving in to his every whim. When his request for a Ferrari was refused, he climbed out of the second-floor window of his home and stood on the ledge, threatening to kill himself unless he got the car. The sisters begged their parents to give their little Pietro what he wanted. The family couldn't afford to lose the last son. He got his Ferrari. That was the kind of guy he was: entitled as all hell and not above terrorist tactics.

All that was back in 1950s Italy. But in the San Diego of the '60s, a southern Italian who barely spoke broken English wasn't exactly considered the cream of the crop. San Diego, which today has seven military bases, has long had a big military presence. The wealth and influence in San Diego has historically been very Republican and very white. Against this backdrop, my dad was the ultimate unwanted outsider.

Americans in stores and restaurants screwed up their faces like they couldn't understand a word he was saying. He was keenly aware that his wool- and silk-blend clothes, which he had tailored to his small frame, looked out of place among the boxy suits and polo shirts and khakis worn by the beefy men around him. His black slicked-back hair elicited taunts from bullies with crew cuts. Once he'd been the central focus of a prominent family, known to all in his town. Now he was a pariah.

Never one to be a victim, however, Jefe decided that *he* was the one who didn't like the kind of people who lived in San Diego. Complaining that they were stuck-up and ignorant, he turned the situation around in a characterization that made him the rejecting party. This reversal allowed him to protect an ego that wouldn't allow him to be vulnerable or to admit that he was hurt by the snubs he experienced.

The good news was that the Mexican border was only a twenty-minute drive away, and he felt *very* comfortable in Tijuana. First of all, he could speak the language—although he spoke the worst Spanish possible. He'd picked it up when the yacht he'd boarded in Rome was forced to anchor in Mexico for several months while the necessary paperwork to reenter the United States was completed. (Back then, if the right amount of money was paid, a ship could dock in Mexico without any paperwork.) As the boat waited for clearance to return to its port of call in Guaymas, a little fishing town off the Sea of Cortez, he literally learned how to swear like a sailor—in Spanish. And he never stopped. No matter how high up in Mexican society he moved later in life, he never lost that way of talking. He spoke with a mouth so foul that many people thought he must be doing it as a joke or a dare. People were constantly saying to me some version of, "I thought your dad was such an asshole, and then I realized he just doesn't know how to speak Spanish."

Although he lived in San Diego, aboard the millionaire's yacht that he'd been employed to manage, Mexican culture felt more like home to my dad than American culture did. He felt comfortable among the men with a similar Latin style, sipping cocktails in the red leather booths of Matteottis, the Italian restaurant in Tijuana where he got to know the city's players.

Still, when the wealthy couple sold their yacht after several years, my father decided to rent a small apartment in San Diego rather than move to TJ. The two cities were so close in proximity that a person could move between them easily for work or just a dinner date, which people did all the time. There was no question for my dad that even if he liked hanging out in Mexico and saw more economic opportunity for himself there, he wanted to *be* an American. He wanted to officially reside in the most powerful country on the globe.

Tijuana in the '60s was a boom time for the Mexican border town. Never one to miss out on an opportunity, Dad got the idea to open a high-end Italian clothing store that catered to Tijuana's elite. From his pals at Matteottis, he'd learned that there was wealth in the dusty city, but for the most part, its inhabitants dressed like shit. Mexican women tended to imitate their richer neighbors to the north, which, in the case of Tijuana and San Diego, had led to the adoption of quite conservative styles. My dad wanted to bring sexy Italian fashion to TJ. Less Macy's and more *La Dolce Vita*. A hustler, he was able to convince the wealthy former yacht owners to give him the seed money to start up a ladies' clothing store, Portofino.

His new boutique in the Colonia Cacho area sold the best clothing Tijuana had ever seen. The who's who of the city flocked to Dad's shop, including many attractive, single, and wealthy young ladies. It didn't take long for him to pivot from an interest in fashion to finding the right woman.

Jefe knew the road to success was faster if he aligned himself with the right family, and he planned to marry into a wealthy one. He was also well into his thirties now, and it was time for him to settle down. Soon he was using the posh clothing store as a lure to attract the most prominent Mexican socialites. Whenever a young woman met his criteria (pretty, rich, and unmarried), he asked her out on a date. By the end of the '60s, he was dating five different socialites at the same time. One of them was my mom.

Nineteen years his junior, Maria Gutierrez was as beautiful, wealthy, and naive as they came. Her father, Fernando Gutierrez, owned and operated one of the largest, if not the largest, customshouse brokerage firms in all of Mexico. He controlled the US-Mexico port of entry between San Diego and Tijuana, the busiest border crossing in the world. From Mexican tomatoes and petroleum that would be sold in the US to farm equipment coming from the US to Mexico, nothing crossed that border without Don Fernando's say-so.

My grandfather was the linchpin in a system that Mexico's major industries—including its biggest supermarket retailers, its oil producers, and its wine exporters—all needed to run smoothly. He grew to be seen as a pillar of the border because people knew they could trust him. His reputation was everything, and he was seen as a man who would never screw anyone over. The majority of his transactions were 100 percent aboveboard. Sure, he might smuggle in an exotic animal for a powerful Mexican's private zoo as a favor, if asked. But he never engaged in nefarious illegal activity like gunrunning, drug trafficking, or human smuggling. Don Fernando was not a criminal but a businessman, and if he happened to look the other way on a shipment of fine

French champagne, he did so only to cement an important business relationship.

In this way, my mother—Maya, as she was called by her family and friends—came from one of the most respected families in the country. She had been groomed at the best private Catholic girls' schools in San Diego: a typical practice for the children of TJ's elite. She was also engaged to a well-to-do young Mexican suitor on the day she walked by Portofino and found, standing outside, "this amazing-looking Italian man smoking a cigarette." This was how she described the moment to me when I was a boy.

Although Jefe never lost the rough shipyard Spanish he picked up in the sleepy Mexican fishing village, he always looked smooth. From the beginning, he favored Brioni suits that flattered his trim five-foot-ten, 180-pound frame. The Italian menswear designer was known for its "Roman" cut: jackets with high armholes, narrow sleeves, and a generally slim—but not tight—fit. Most stocky Mexican men could only dream of fitting into the body-conscious suits, one of which Marcello Mastroianni wore in director Federico Fellini's 1960 film, *La Dolce Vita*.

No wonder my mother's first image of my dad was that of a movie star: hair slicked back, smoking a cigarette, wearing a black-and-white-checkered blazer, black pants, and perfect shoes. She *instantly fell in love*. As for her fiancé, Maya decided she wasn't really attracted to him. Her parents had set up the union, and she had gone along with it. But once she saw my dad, she decided she didn't want a boy; she wanted a man. My mom said, "I just looked at him and knew he was going to be my husband."

Portofino was my dad's honeypot to lure socialites, and my mother—or as I called her, Ama—was TJ's most prized catch. Not only did she come from a wealthy and stable family—two qualities that don't always go hand in hand—she also was beautiful. She wore her glossy black hair so long it hit her waist. My dad was a sucker for high heels and a great pair of legs, and my mother had both. She loved the way

13

her legs looked in heels so much, she would have fallen asleep in them if she could. On top of all her other qualities, my mother had received a top education in the US. A good student, she could speak Spanish and English fluently and without an accent.

Still, my dad wasn't putting all his eggs in one basket. My mother was just one of five women he was dating at the time. Mom might have been young, but she wasn't stupid. She knew he was a player. So she made her own move. "If you're serious about me, Pietro, you're going to hire my good friend Angelo," she said. "If not, we won't date anymore."

Angelo Serena was one of my mom's best friends, and she wanted him to be her eyes and ears in the store. My father gave in to her demand, and Angelo wound up becoming his right-hand man—and staying so long after the store was gone. Angelo and my father proved their loyalty to one another early on. Both my mom and dad would tell me the following story. The facts of it always pissed my mom off. Telling the story always put a smile on my dad's face.

Whenever she called the store, whoever answered knew who she was and called her by name. So how, she wondered, could Pietro be seeing anyone else? Wouldn't the sales staff get her name mixed up sometimes and call her by the name of one of his other girlfriends? Or even worse, ask, *Which girlfriend?* That never happened. She was always greeted as if everyone knew exactly who she was.

Yet, she had a feeling. Finally, Angelo admitted the secret methodology. "There's a board," said my mother's friend. He was supposed to have been protecting her interests, but my dad already had him wrapped around his finger. Angelo was young, the same age as my mom, and he looked up to Jefe like he was the coolest guy on the planet. In return for this devotion, my dad had been helping Angelo with his clothes and with women, and was turning him into a stud.

"What do you mean, there's a board?" my mother asked.

"There's a board with the names of each of his girlfriends, what they typically say when they call, and other ways to tell them apart."

She stormed into Portofino in a rage, demanding, "Where is the fucking board? I want to see it." A scared saleswoman pointed at an area where a stack of boxes stood. Mom pulled a box to the side, and there was a board with the names of each woman; a few biographical details for each to help the worker figure out which girlfriend they were speaking to; and instructions on how to greet each woman so that the boss would know which one was on the other end of the line.

That day, my mom delivered an ultimatum: "It's either me or these other women."

My dad committed to dating my mom exclusively, and they began what was a proper courtship for Mexico at that time. Primarily, that meant they didn't sleep together—at least not right away. She held out for more than a year, but their attraction to one another was very strong. Finally, she gave in to her urges and his, and wound up pregnant. After that, there was no other option but for them to marry. Ama was twenty-one years old and still in her first trimester when she married my dad on August 2, 1970. Only family—about sixty in all—were invited to the intimate ceremony that was held at my grandparents' house in Tijuana. Though it was customary to marry in a church, my grandfather was ashamed that his daughter had become pregnant out of wedlock to El Italiano, whose colorful shirts and snug pants made Abuelo question the Italian's manhood. In his mind, she had disrespected the Catholic Church and the family. In rejecting the husband her father had wanted for her, my mother had made her own choice: to be no longer under my grandfather's control.

Though she'd acted with the brashness of youth in going after this older, foreign man, my mother carried the guilt of their sin for the rest of her life. Whenever we went to church, she never took the Eucharist. As a child, I pressed her on it, and she claimed that it was because she hadn't "obeyed the Church's rules on procreation."

"I didn't have a second or third child," she said, "and the Church says you should do your best to procreate as much as possible."

As a child, I believed her. Years later, though, I realized she had been lying to me because she *had* tried to have another baby. She'd told me when I got older that she had suffered a miscarriage that prevented her from trying any further. I didn't revisit the issue of the holy sacrament after that realization, however. I didn't want to press her.

I simply think she never took communion again because she was ashamed.

∼

Like most children of moneyed Tijuana families, I was born in the United States even though my parents were still living in Tijuana. In my case, it happened on April 22, 1971, at Scripps Memorial Hospital in the La Jolla neighborhood of San Diego. My mother and her brother had both been born a twenty-minute drive away at Scripps Mercy, also in San Diego. Although the medical facilities were, in fact, better on the US side of the border, the real draw to having one's children born in the United States was dual citizenship. Being born in San Diego immediately entitled children from Tijuana to US citizenship, while our heritage and land entitled us to a Mexican passport as well.

Unfortunately, getting Mexican passports the honest way was a long, involved process. But as the guy who controlled the border, my grandfather knew everybody involved in border patrol and customs. Because of this, he was able to get documentation that claimed my mother, my uncle, and I had been born in Mexico. Why wait, Grandpa rationalized, when you can circumvent the laws and get it done in a day? Especially when wait time is the only factor that will change, and a positive result is ensured.

Because so many of us in my family had dual citizenship, the border was nothing more than an arbitrary line for us. But the money our dual citizenship made for my grandfather and many others was very real. Yes, the border divided two different cultures—one that purportedly prized law and order; the other where corruption was a wholly acceptable tool for those who were lucky enough to afford it.

My parents' move from my grandparents' home in Tijuana to Bonita in Southern San Diego is just one example of how our chosen sides of the border changed in order to suit our circumstances. Eight months after my parents' shotgun wedding, there was a problem at the house in Tijuana. The water wasn't flowing properly, so Jefe and Abuelo went out to the well, which had been drained to allow them to locate the source of the obstruction. While inspecting it, my dad saw four rats at the bottom.

Jefe was a meticulous man in all things. When he dressed, everything from his tie to his shoes had to be perfect. He cared a great deal about cleanliness, and he feared germs.

"I can't live with this," he declared. "It's not safe for my family or me."

It wasn't just the quality of the well water that was substandard but the general lower level of sanitary conditions in Mexico that was inferior to conditions just across the border.

My father decided to move our family of three to Bonita, about ten minutes north of the border. San Diego is divided into three parts: Southern San Diego, Central, and Northern. Bonita was located in the south, which is a predominantly Hispanic area. When you go south of the Coronado Bridge, you had better be prepared to speak Spanish because English is the second language there. At the time of our move, my father still owned Portofino in Tijuana. He was still close to work after our move, but he also felt more comfortable in Bonita.

The house had a big backyard and a pool, and we were all comfortable living there. But now Jefe had a problem: he had a household to support. His plan to marry rich had backfired, because, frankly, my grandfather didn't like my dad. Before Jefe and Ama wed, Abuelo said, "Pietro, you will never get your hands on one penny of my money or on anything the Gutierrez family owns."

Now, two years into my parents' marriage, Jefe needed money. Portofino was still the place for the well-heeled woman in TJ to shop. My grandmother adored the store. My mom loved accompanying my dad on his buying trips to Italy, and she loved that she was better dressed than any other woman because of her husband. The shop might have been good fun for them. Instead, for my dad, it was a source of stress. There was not enough wealth in TJ to sustain the kind of client base he needed to make a living. The margins were just too tight.

So my dad, whose opportunistic nature allowed him to sense the opportunism in others, too, hatched a plan that he described to me as soon as I was old enough to understand. This is the story that always followed one of his favorite sayings: the one about never asking a man how he made his first million.

I don't know if Jefe actually made a million by doing what he did with Portofino, but this is how he made money for a while: he committed insurance fraud. He wasn't stupid enough to do it on his own. For him to do it right—that is, to get away with it—he had to pull into the scam the very people whose job it would be to catch him. So he propositioned the police and fire chiefs as well as the insurance adjuster, and he got them to see his side of things by explaining how much money they all stood to make. Faced with a promised payday that exceeded two years' worth of paychecks, these officials agreed to join with my father and become their own little criminal network.

Burning down Portofino was easy money. The fire chief prepped my father, explaining in detail, from top to bottom, all that he needed to know to carry out the arson. Once my father was ready, he doused some clothes near an electrical outlet with lighter fluid, threw a lit cigarette on them, and hightailed it out of there. He did it on a night when both the fire and police chief were on duty, so that they'd be the first ones on scene to field any questions that came up or to collect—and disappear—any evidence he might have left behind.

Afterward, the insurance adjuster assessed the building's value at four times its real value. After Dad recouped his original investment in the business, the four men split the rest of the claim money. Then my dad sold the land, for a nice little double-dip.

It was so easy, the men couldn't stop there. They identified other properties in TJ ripe for arson. One at a time, my dad purchased a property, using some of his earnings from the previous fire. After some time had passed, he would burn it down like he had Portofino. After they'd rinsed and repeated four times, the scam grew a little obvious, even for a city with as much corruption as TJ.

The thing is, TJ is really just a small town masking as a city, and word gets around. It didn't take long for the gossip of my dad's scheme to make its way back to Abuelo, who was shaken by the news. My grandfather was a man of respect, both in that he commanded respect and valued it as quality. He had never liked my father, but this was far worse. He couldn't imagine having a criminal for a son-in-law. He confronted my mother.

"Maya, you need to leave him," he said.

"I can't," she said. "I made a commitment to him."

"Come to me. I'll adopt Picho as my own," said my grandfather. He was referring to me by my nickname—a Mexican takeoff on *piscione*, Italian for "pisser," a name I earned because my abuela said I peed and pooed a lot.

"I can't."

"Pietro is a bad man. He will taint the family name."

But although she herself was upset by my father's crimes, my mother could not bring herself to leave him.

"Papa," she said. "I love him."

CHAPTER 2

On Abuelo's Ranch

One of the ranch hands opened up the massive iron gate so that the car carrying my grandfather, grandmother, and me could pass.

"Welcome to Fantasy Island!" I said, parroting Ricardo Montalbán's catchphrase from one of my favorite TV shows, *Fantasy Island*. To my grandparents' delight, I delivered the pronouncement in a fair impression of Montalbán's gravelly Hispanic accent, even though I was just eight. The line always came at the moment of the show when the guests, stepping foot on the island for the first time, were bowled over by its majesty. This was the same awe I always felt upon arriving at Rancho San Fernando, my grandparents' two-hundred-acre property near the sleepy beach town of Rosarito, twenty-five miles south of TJ.

Once we were through the gate, Abuelo drove his white Ford Mercury Crown Victoria station wagon up the quarter-mile cobblestone driveway that led to the main house. My grandfather was a car guy, but imported vehicles less than five years old were too expensive for even Mexico's elite, because the import taxes on new foreign cars in Mexico could be as high as double their value. For that reason, new foreign cars were too conspicuous to drive.

Driving a new Mercedes was, in fact, tantamount to putting a target on your back. Plus, my grandfather reasoned, a nice car like that would just get ruined on the rough country roads that led to the ranch anyway. The made-in-Mexico Crown Vic station wagon also had the space he needed, since he was always transporting riding gear and other stuff from his office to the ranch.

The driveway to the ranch was lined with a collection of vintage cars and carriages: evidence of his passion for vehicles. There were three 1950s convertible Cadillacs—one in green, another in white, and a third in red, all with fins—representing the national colors of Mexico. However, it was the horse-drawn carriages he had on display that were his real babies. The carriages married his love of horses and history. The antiques from the turn of the twentieth century evoked the opulence of a bygone era that he hoped the ranch offered. He wanted to transport people back in time from the moment they got to the driveway.

We entered the roundabout that led to the entrance of the house. It was decorated with a dozen or more flags that hung from flagpoles and whipped in the wind that came from the Pacific Ocean, right below the house. A history buff, Abuelo collected flags from all over the world. Of course, the US, Canada, and Mexico were represented, but so were many countries in Europe. If Abuelo had a guest from abroad, he would raise the flag of their country. If he didn't already have that particular flag, he would buy it. He even had a flag made from a family crest he'd designed, which was decorated with a mix of Aztec and Spanish symbols.

As we approached, most of the ranch's twenty staff members stood in front of the massive twelve-foot-high tiered stone fountain in the middle of the roundabout, waiting to greet us. The water in the fountain gurgled calmly as it cascaded into a large and ornate basin.

Javier, the tall, thin ranch caretaker in his twenties, bowed slightly. He offered a courteous hand to my grandmother as she exited the car. Two other staff members grabbed our bags from the trunk. All twenty of the men wore the same uniform: a gray jumpsuit like the kind golf caddies wear, with "Rancho San Fernando" stitched in green thread at the breast. It was like arriving at a five-star hotel.

From the time I had first begun school, I had been shipped off from our house in Bonita to my grandparents' place in Tijuana every Friday afternoon, like clockwork. My grandfather, who ended work around the same time I finished school, would come pick me up after the bus dropped me off at home. I would spend Friday nights in front of the TV, tended to by my grandparents' housekeeper in TJ, while they went on their weekly date. The next morning, the three of us would be off to Rancho San Fernando.

Only forty minutes from their house in Tijuana, the ranch boasted an Olympic-size pool, tennis and basketball courts, and even its own chapel, where I was baptized as a baby and later took my first communion. My grandfather hosted business associates and their families, so there were usually kids to play with or some other fun going on. However, for those who loved to ride—like my grandfather, uncle, and me—the real draw of the ranch was horseback riding. The ranch was home to the Club Hipico San Fernando, the riding club for Tijuana's socialites, where the city's most influential families came for lessons in English riding.

The stables contained anywhere between thirty and forty horses. Five pros taught jumping and dressage, as well as organized show days and competitions that ran throughout the entire year. The ranch's two hundred acres, which traversed both oceanfronts and mountain ranges, provided the backdrop to long horseback rides that took us from stretches of white sandy beaches to rugged hills green with scrub oak. Like I said, Fantasy Island.

The rise in reputation of Rancho San Fernando as a top-notch riding club mirrored my grandfather's expansion of the business he'd inherited from his father, who was one of the first men in Mexico to get a customshouse broker's license. The license my great-grandfather obtained in the 1920s allowed him to process the paperwork necessary to import any goods coming into Mexico from abroad. That license guaranteed wealth.

The elder brother of two more brothers and a sister—Fausto, Fidel, and Flor—Fernando Gutierrez Moreno had taken on the leadership role at the customs agency long before their father died. The three strapping guys, who were as much good friends as they were brothers, supported one another in all things. So much so that because Fausto was the sole distributor of RC Cola for all Mexico, Fernando never allowed Coca-Cola to be served on his ranch—not even long after Fausto had died.

It was Fausto's death that ultimately caused a rift between my grandfather and Fidel. A much-beloved man, not just in the family but also in all of Tijuana, Fausto died in his late forties from a massive coronary. (The city renamed the central gym after my great-uncle who, standing at six foot four, had been an avid basketball player.) The traumatic loss destabilized the relationship among the remaining siblings. Contention rose over which brother was better equipped to run the customs business eventually, and Fausto, the peacemaker, was no longer there to calm the hot tempers of Fidel and my grandfather. When my great-grandfather left his license to his firstborn after his death, the divide between the brothers was complete.

My abuelo inherited the customs brokerage not just because of birth order, however. His father also had seen that his oldest son had the vision and the drive for the brokerage business. The building my grandfather subsequently constructed along the border was a symbol of both those qualities. Finished in 1958, the building was so modern, it looked like it belonged on a Manhattan street and not the dusty crossing on which it stood.

The US Customs building that currently sits two feet away from my grandfather's building was finished in the early '60s and has one floor; my grandfather's has four. He knew that constructing a building of that magnitude would give him a strong presence at the border and put him in a good position to succeed. And it did. As the head of the number one customs brokerage in Mexico, Don Fernando controlled nearly all the goods crossing the border from the time he built the building until his death.

Indeed, presence got Abuelo far, and not just at the border. He established Rancho San Fernando in the 1950s outside of Rosarito by squatting on the two hundred acres, which was just as hard as it sounds. Cars were scarce then in Rosarito, which was, during those years, just a small sleepy town and not the spring break party mecca it would become decades later. My grandfather hired workers to build a fence around the perimeter of the property. Then he dispatched the staff he'd hired to work at the ranch to patrol and protect that fence line—much like border agents.

Usually my grandfather was busy with his customs business, but he loved to ride out to the farthest corners with the ranch hands, his six-shooter in his holster. He didn't want anyone messing with his land. This was some Wild West, Pancho Villa shit. Just like the European settlers who pushed west across the United States, this is how it was done at the time in Mexico. After a period of time, my grandfather went to the municipality and officially claimed the land for his own. The government official who signed the papers was handsomely rewarded in cash.

The main house of the ranch was relatively simple. With only three bedrooms, it was not meant as a place for visitors to stay overnight. Still, it had a regal air, with a grand entrance that boasted a forty-foot ceiling and a twelve-foot-wide fireplace with portraits of the family flanking both sides. There was a dining room set back from the entrance, but it was never used after Abuelo had a solarium built with sliding glass doors that opened right out to a glorious view of the ocean. As if that weren't dramatic enough, he commissioned a special dining room table that could seat up to forty people. On Saturday nights, guests would walk outside to the wraparound porch to line up near the grill, heap their plates with carne asada, and bring it back to the table.

Rancho San Fernando wasn't a moneymaking enterprise. But that didn't mean it wasn't about business. Politicians, industrialists, import-exporters, socialites—those important to his customshouse business and those they wanted to be around—were all taken care of while at the ranch. It was *the* place to be on the weekend thanks to my grandfather's legendary graciousness and meticulous oversight, which began every Saturday at eight o'clock in the morning.

After we'd arrived at the ranch bright and early, the first thing Abuelo would do was check on the more than thirty horses, which were all saddled up by the ranch hand Roberto.

"Pichito, come," he would say to me as we entered the stables to check every horse, every leg and tendon, to make sure the guests would not be subjected to any stumbles.

Abuelo's own horse was a large and beautiful white mare, which he rode sitting with the straightest posture I've ever seen. Up on his English saddle—one hand holding both reins, the other hand on his hip—he was the very picture of his idol, Napoleon Bonaparte. My grandfather admired how the French leader had risen through the military ranks to seize power and conquer much of Europe. Plus, Abuelo loved Napoleon's over-the-top style. My grandfather loved regalia of all kinds, from the international flags hanging from flagpoles that lined the entrance of the estate to marching bands.

How he loved a marching band! On show days, he would have riders of all ages from the equestrian center file in, marching band music playing in the background as they paraded in circles in front of all the guests. I participated in the pageant going back as far as I can remember, since my grandfather had me atop a horse at two years old, seated in a custom-made saddle he'd designed for me.

The saddle was like a tiny car seat that sat atop the horse. It even had a seat belt. Strapped into my saddle, I was pulled around by one of the ranch hands. From the very beginning, I loved the feeling of being on a horse. By age five, I was jumping my first hurdles and a year later competing on five-foot hurdles. I became an excellent rider thanks to my grandfather, who taught me everything I needed to know about horsemanship—and more than I ever needed to know about Napoleon.

Once he was satisfied with the condition of the horses, Abuelo would take me on a ride with him around the property to continue his inspection. After that, we returned to the ranch to see how the food and drink preparations were going. Finally, the guests began to arrive. Anyone who would be riding had to be at the ranch by 10:00 a.m. When a guest showed up, that's when Abuelo's love for pomp and circumstance went on full display.

It was just like a scene in the movies when guests are announced at a royal ball: "Lord So-and-So from Such-and-Such!" With Abuela and me by his side, Abuelo would greet each visitor with his characteristic flair. He kissed the hands of the female guests and clicked his heels. The men received one kiss on each cheek and a hug on the right side, as was the custom at the time in Mexico.

The big show we put on to welcome guests was the first of many details in his plan for them all to have a phenomenal time while at the ranch.

If visitors came on a weekend when there wasn't an equestrian show, those of us who wanted to saddled up for a long ride along the beach. On hot days, we rode the horses into the ocean right up to our thighs. Other times, we took a daylong trip to the mountains on the outskirts of Rosarito. We rode the horses to Cerro El Coronel, then on to the other peak of El Coronel. A staff of four would ride ahead and wait for us at a lunch site midmountain. Over the fire, they cooked the steak and heated up the rice, beans, and homemade tortillas for a lunch of Bistec Ranchero. Guests would take a tortilla, stuff it with the delicious hot fillings, and eat it right out of their hands. No plates necessary. The simplicity of a taco eaten beside your horse with the Pacific glinting in view from fifteen miles away is pure magic. I swelled with pride as I flanked Abuelo. Sitting erect upon his white horse, he gazed out at the green mountains and azure sea as if he owned them.

The guests who didn't ride horses had plenty to keep them occupied as well. They were invited to enjoy the pool, which was located past a large lawn, in its own area with a pool house and a bar with a Ping-Pong table. Behind the bar were the tennis courts, and behind them, the ocean. There were also dirt bikes and all-terrain vehicles available to those who wanted to explore the ranch or just have fun getting really dirty.

One never knew who might be at the ranch on any given weekend. Many guests were clients of the customs business, like the owner of Calimax, a supermarket chain, whose trucks carrying imported food my grandfather helped cross from Tijuana to San Diego. A separate house to the right of the ranch, called "the office," was basically one big square room with a conference table and three oversize desks. Here, guests, like the mayor of TJ—who came to the ranch often with his family—went to play cards or have a private conversation. One wall of the office was built from the wood of trees that had been cut lengthwise into slabs. If you pulled up one of the slabs, it opened on to a secret Chinese garden with a small pond and a little red bridge. The office was the perfect place to have impromptu discussions.

Members of the Estudillo, Fimbres, and Trevino families—high-society types who were interested in riding and having fun—were regular visitors. There was also the occasional American. My grandfather schmoozed a few executives and producers from Hollywood who were thinking about filming in TJ and Rosarito to save money. He wound up importing all the goods for the production company that shot one of the Herbie the Love Bug movies, *Herbie Goes Bananas*. I even appeared in a scene that was filmed at the bullring in Playas de Tijuana after Abuelo invited me to come check out the shoot.

Although my grandfather's generosity could reap personal rewards, his motivation for entertaining wasn't craven. He genuinely lived by the motto *mi casa es su casa*. When guests invariably remarked on what a wonderful time they'd had at the ranch, he always said, "Come whenever you want. My doors are always open." (And they did; people were always showing up out of the blue.) He was the type of guy who, if someone complimented his tie, would take the tie off and give it to the person. This was much to the chagrin of Abuela, who picked out his equestrian-themed Hermès ties and knew just how expensive they were, even if he did not.

He handed down his flair for hospitality like a birthright. Years later, when I was in middle school in San Diego, my mother invited the entire faculty from my private school to spend a day at the ranch and eat a massive carne asada. The teachers and administration fell in love with my family. I'll never forget the image of my sixth-grade teacher driving a dune buggy with mud all over her face, wearing a smile from ear to ear. That year, my family's hospitality earned me a little extra grace at school, where my behavior and grades weren't exactly perfect.

Everyone should enjoy the ranch. Nowhere was my abuelo's mantra more on display than during Saturday-night dinners. The evening festivities began around four o'clock, as the guests started to meander back to the estate from their various activities. Plentiful appetizers and drinks were laid out to nibble on and sip. As people enjoyed the tail end of the day with their beverages of choice, the aroma of the most delicious carne asada you ever smelled wafted through the balmy air.

The promise of dinner eventually beckoned the visitors to the table, which could be configured for a smaller group of ten or up to the full forty, depending on the number of guests. The vibrant pinks and oranges of the sun setting over the darkening jewel of the sea had to compete with platters of out-of-this-world food for the diners' attention. Abuelo had some of the best people cooking for him. One of them was Teresita. Though only four feet nine inches tall, the woman was a force of nature, and her homemade flour tortillas—the same ones heated up over the fire mountainside for lunch tacos—were legendary. They melted in your mouth. At Christmastime, friends of my grand-parents also clamored for her *buñuelos*: fried dough topped with sugar. Every dish at the dinners was special—even the rice and beans, which Teresita would flavor with chorizo, bacon fat, chicken broth, or melted cheese. Teresita had previously been my mother's nanny, and she also managed my grandparents' household. But cooking was her pride. So when Anita, who'd been hired to work under Teresita, stole the show one night with an American flag made of Jell-O dish for a Fourth of July celebration, there were fireworks not just out on the lawn but also in the kitchen.

Occasionally, the food came from other places. Sometimes Abuelo would pay to close down a restaurant in Puerto Nuevo, the "lobster capital of Baja," and have the staff prepare for the ranch heaps and heaps of lobster so tender, the shell came right off with the merest touch of a fork. Regardless of who'd done the cooking, as the sun went down, the French wine flowed, and the food kept coming. Abuelo hired musicians to perform when dessert was served, either a good Mexican-style guitar-ist or a mariachi band. To my young mind, these dinner parties seemed to go on forever. Sometimes they did stretch into the graying of the sky that occurred not long before dawn. Saturday was Don Fernando's day to let loose. He was proud: he had a magnificent ranch, a large professional staff. He'd provided a beautiful meal. He was *el rey*. That was Don Fernando at his best.

Then came Don Fernando at his worst. After the festivities, Abuelo, drunk enough that he could hardly walk, insisted on driving home. Although he could sleep at the ranch, he always wanted to go home, like the rest of his guests, and sleep in his own bed—even if that meant returning to the ranch the next day. But before we could drive back, we needed to make it back to the city, and that was no small feat.

All this happened in the years before the new freeway was built. Back then, the ride from Rosarito to Tijuana—forty white-knuckling treacherous minutes—took place on old, winding single-lane roads. Always in that minute after we'd passed a truck and were driving toward an oncoming car, before scooting back into our own lane, I prayed silently, *Don't let us die. Don't let us die . . .*

Abuela and I would remain silent the whole excruciating journey home. Yes, Abuelo was wasted. However, he was also the man of the house. If he wanted to drive back to Tijuana, then he was going to drive back to Tijuana. There was nothing either of us could do. This was complicated by the fact that my grandmother didn't drive—and not because she didn't know how.

Once when I was older, my grandfather leveled with me and told me that he'd married my grandmother because she was beautiful and because she never questioned him. He'd met Irma Scollari—a beauty queen from Calexico and a second-generation Italian-Mexican on her mother's side—when she was vying for the title of Miss Baja California at a competition in Tijuana's legendary jai alai (a form of handball native to the Basque region of Spain) venue. Theirs was a pretty simple love story. Smitten by her classic Italian looks, just as my mother would one day become smitten with my father's, he fell in love. Although she was a horrible cook and never cleaned a single thing in her life—thankfully, they had four people on staff in Tijuana to do all that—Grandpa called her "the perfect wife."

Part of that perfection involved staying in her lane. Grandma wanted to look good, which she did to the end of her days. She never changed her look: Yves Saint Laurent and Escada silk dresses that fell just below the knee, heels, coiffed hair in the style of an '80s socialite, and impeccable makeup. She was the picture of elegance. The only thing about her that changed over the years was that she let her hair go gray.

She cared about appearances of all kinds. The house was immaculate, with everything in its place at all times. She expected flawless manners at her table. My goodness, she was a stickler for perfection. She taught me how to eat according to rules of etiquette considered proper not just in the United States and South America but in Europe as well. Man, if I swapped my fork and knife hand or an elbow went on the table, my butt paid the price. My grandmother was a spanker, and her discipline had the desired effect. I have impeccable manners to this day. Back then, I felt awful when I disappointed my grandmother, but I don't remember her punishments as traumatic. Although my grandfather never spanked me, spanking as punishment was the norm at the time.

Just as my grandfather's life ran by a precise schedule, so did my grandmother's. Abuelo's schedule revolved around work; hers centered on keeping everything—herself included—beautiful and her man happy. Ever since I could remember, my mom and grandma had gotten their hair and nails done every Thursday for a date night on Friday. One of Abuela's most prized possessions was a knuckle-to-knuckle emerald ring: a gift from my grandfather that she wore at all times. Often she matched her fingernail polish to the ring. Grandma loved her green nails. My mom's were ruby red all the time.

Having been picked up by my grandfather on Friday afternoon and brought to the house in TJ, per our weekly routine, I would watch, fully ensconced in a La-Z-Boy–style chair in front of the TV, as my grandmother came downstairs all dolled up. She would instruct the staff to make me a big hot-fudge sundae, and then she would set out to parade in on Abuelo's arm to one of the restaurants where Tijuana society went to be seen and where she could enjoy her very cold Beefeater martini, up with an olive.

Abuela knew her lane; she *loved* her lane. She wore her traditional role as a badge of honor, even using it to mask a terrible tragedy from early on in her marriage. Shortly after she was married, my grandfather had bought my grandmother her first car, and she'd killed a man as he was crossing the street. She was never charged. (Continual gifts and donations to those up and down the ladder of the criminal justice system meant the rules did not apply to our family.) But the man's death weighed heavy on her. For a long while, she didn't even like riding in a car.

At first, Abuelo tried to convince her to drive again, but she was too scared. Over the years the narrative drifted, so that the story was no longer that she'd been scarred by the psychological trauma of killing a man. The story now told was that my grandfather *wanted* her to have a driver because this was befitting for the wife of an important man. Whichever of these explanations was closer to true, she never drove again. This is why my grandmother and I were left to suffer through my grandfather's drunk driving when we came home late at night from the ranch.

We should have died, riding in the car with him when he was in that condition, and more than a few times, we almost did. Driving in Mexico was a totally different and much more aggressive experience than in the US. Sometimes my grandfather's head would literally be nodding into his chin, the car swerving, until my grandmother elbowed him awake again. Other times, alcohol made Abuelo overconfident in his abilities. On the two-lane road, he passed cars on frightening curves in circumstances when even professional drivers would have known better than to try.

Such was the case when we were coming home from the ranch one Saturday night when I was seven and we got stuck behind a semi. Feeling impatient, Abuelo decided to pass the truck on the left side while going around a bend. The moment we reached the truck's side, we saw coming straight at us another big truck that he hadn't seen because of the curve. My grandmother screamed as Abuelo gunned the engine. The oncoming truck swerved into the side of the road, which only gave our car two feet of extra room. Somehow, there was just enough space for my grandfather to squeeze between the semis, narrowly escaping being crushed to death.

That near miss was too terrifying for me to forget. As my mother tucked me into bed that Sunday evening, I said, "I don't want to go back to the ranch anymore." That didn't make sense to her. She did a little digging, and soon I was recounting the incident in tears. Finally, my mother had had it. She decided that Abuelo *needed* a driver to take us home. But Ama knew better than to overtly force the issue, as this would only prompt her proud father to dig in his heels. Instead, she suggested that he hire someone who could take care of me when he was busy entertaining his guests *and* drive us home after a long, exhausting day. She also had the perfect person in mind: Germán.

Germán was Teresita's twenty-three-year-old son-in-law. The unassuming man with dark curly hair and that thick mustache standard for Mexican men of the day had just married Teresita's daughter, Cookie. Later, they would go on to have three sons: Alex, Bebbo, and Carlitos. My mom convinced Abuelo that Germán was an honest, hardworking man who would look after me and keep me entertained. The fact that he could then drive us home from the ranch at night as well was simply a bonus. My grandfather agreed, and Germán was hired.

A very good soccer player and all-around athlete, Germán taught me how to play all kinds of sports, including American sports like baseball and basketball. In between the two tasks of entertaining me and driving us home from the ranch, he also ran errands for my grandparents. One of the hardest-working people I have ever known, he always kept busy and never talked badly about anyone. In fact, he didn't talk much at all. He simply kept his head down and got the job done. On Friday afternoons when I got out of school, I was always happy to see Germán.

I would have never guessed he would wind up the ultimate family confidence man, holding the secrets that belonged to my grandfather, my father, and my uncle—and eventually, the secrets that belonged to me.

CHAPTER 3

"Where There Is Devastation, There Is Opportunity"

One morning when I was eight, my grandfather came to the dining room table in Tijuana looking a little worse for wear. As was his practice whenever he was hungover from a big Saturday dinner at the ranch, he drank down the *menudo* the maid placed before him. The pungent steaming bowl of tripe stewed in chiles that had been toasted, soaked, and blended into the broth was spicy as hell. *Menudo* was also hailed in Mexico as a cure for a night of heavy drinking.

Abuelo sweated and cried as he ate the bright-red soup. But after that, he was ready to roll, and off my grandparents and I went in the Crown Vic for another day at the ranch—although Sunday was always a shorter day because he had to be up on Monday morning at 4:00 a.m.

Don Fernando was the anomaly among middle- and upper-middle-class married men in Mexico who—long after that lifestyle had gone out of vogue with its neighbor to the north—stayed out drinking until all hours of the night without needing to check in with their spouses. His work had him at the office before customs opened in the morning and out by 3:30 in the afternoon, a half hour after customs shut down for direct droppings. Home by four, he ate dinner a half hour later, watched the news and maybe a little sports, and was fast asleep by 8:00 p.m. The only "sleeping in" he did was on weekends, when he awoke at seven to get ready for a day at the ranch.

Abuelo's regimented schedule was the polar opposite of my father's. Jefe was the typical Latin guy who stayed at work late and then went out to eat with his cronies, not returning home until long after my bedtime. He got to do whatever he wanted while the woman stayed at home. But if my mom had any problems with the arrangement, I was never aware of them. Ama seemed perfectly content to wait for the bus to drop me off from school, eat dinner together, and then watch TV with me on the couch. We spent all our time together during the weekdays. My mom was my best friend.

Then, on the weekends, it was back to the ranch, where my dad did not like to spend time. He didn't fit in there. The first problem was his clothes. Dad didn't know how to dress "ranch." At the big parties my grandparents occasionally held there, he looked great in his usual perfectly tailored Italian suit and immaculate shoes. He would be the best-looking guy there—and know it. But he couldn't wear a pair of jeans to save his life. Years later, when he and my uncle were embroiled in a development project on the ranch, my dad decided that he needed to be present and physically involved in the construction as the workers put up a fence around the site. He decided I needed to be there, too, so he could show me what manual labor was all about. But he didn't dress properly for the role, so it took great effort for me not to laugh as I watched him, dressed in his Canali slacks and wearing shiny Italian loafers, drive stakes into the dirt.

If he was going to his store, he would be dressed in a suit and tie. Out to dinner? A suit and tie. On the ranch? Suit and tie. The man liked to be in a suit and tie. Appearances were very important to my father. He taught me: "When you have no money, that's the time to spend. Even if you're down to your last two cents, you should always look good." To do otherwise would be a sign of weakness. Maybe that's why he sent me off to my first day of kindergarten in a fucking suit and tie. Everyone else was wearing OP shorts like normal San Diego kids. I showed up looking like an accountant.

Starting a new school was hard enough. My outfit only made things worse. I felt so out of place sweating in my suit. Some of the kids laughed at me as I slid around in my dress shoes while trying to run on the school playground. Humiliated, I came home crying.

Jefe was not moved. The next day, he made me do it all again, dressed in the suit, tie, and dress shoes. His obsession with appearances, like so many other things, stemmed from the deep insecurity he'd internalized after his broken English and status as an immigrant had made him feel undesirable during his first years in America. At the time, I didn't realize the indelible mark this experience had left on him. I just saw him as a hard man who was not to be trifled with.

Dad thought money was the way to overcome all his insecurities. He assumed the nicest, most expensive clothes signified wealth and importance. Eventually, he relented on the suit, allowing me to wear a polo shirt and tailored shorts instead. But even then, he still made me wear dress shoes to school every day.

"Tennis shoes are meant for tennis," he yelled when I tried to revisit the issue, "and they're going to ruin your feet."

Tennis shoes are so much more comfortable; how can they ruin your feet? I kept that thought to myself until my next visit to the pediatrician, and then I brought the subject up with the doctor.

"No, sneakers and regular shoes act just the same," he said. "As long as they are your size, they won't hurt your feet."

Satisfied, I looked over at my mom. She didn't look nearly as happy as I felt because she was the one who was going to have to deal with this at home.

Later that night, she told my father a variation on the truth: "The doctor said he doesn't know what shoes are better or not. But psychologically speaking, you'd better buy him tennis shoes. Because if everyone's wearing tennis shoes and he's the only one not wearing tennis shoes, he's going to be excluded. He's not going to be part of the group, and that will hurt him."

My dad took me to Sears and bought me nine pairs of sneakers the very next day.

My father didn't just use appearances as a way to seek acceptance. He also weaponized the issue, particularly in his relationship with my mother. Normally she dressed to his taste, which was stuck in the fashions he'd featured at the high-end women's clothing store he opened during the '60s. Usually a silk dress that hit right below the knee with high heels and her hair pulled back. Very conservative. While her look was elegant, it also aged her.

One time, though, my mother and I went out shopping, and she decided to try something a little more current. She bought a pair of leather pants that she paired with an elegant blouse and high heels. That evening, she took extra time getting ready to go out with my father. It was a big night for Jefe, who had some new business connections he wanted to impress.

When my mother finally came out of the bedroom, she was the very picture of current glamor. She was dressed in her new expensive leather pants and beautiful flowing silk blouse. Her thick black hair was pulled back, revealing a heavy gold necklace that matched her earrings, and her makeup was immaculate. She looked like a classier version of Olivia Newton-John in *Grease*.

"Pinche puta!" my father roared.

His words—*fucking whore*—hit her like a sucker punch, hard and out of the blue.

"Take that crap off," he seethed.

She looked nothing like a prostitute, but my father's cruelty had exactly the effect he'd intended. My mom, tears of shame running down her cheeks and ruining her makeup, ran back into the bedroom to change.

I wish I could say this was a one-off event, but my dad often lost his temper over my mother's clothes. Sometimes, like in the case of the leather pants, he complained that her outfits were too revealing. Other times, he said they weren't revealing enough. His anger wasn't about fashion; it was about his controlling nature. If he didn't choose an outfit, she didn't get to wear it.

My father's anger took a different form when it came to me. I received the full fury of his wrath whenever I fell or bumped into something. He didn't care about the usual things parents care about, like if I'd done my homework or whether my grades were slipping. Such matters were not even on my dad's radar. But if I broke a glass or tripped over a chair, out came the belt. Even if it wasn't my fault.

One display of his anger involved my dog Misty. Our family had three German shepherds that had all flunked the police test. Though they hadn't made the squad, they were the best-trained pets on earth.

Misty was my dog. She slept in my bed and played with me. She was even able to jump up and hit the tetherball back to me. One day, I had been playing tetherball with her when, having decided I was done, I turned to walk away. Misty, who was clearly not done playing, came up from behind and jumped on my back, pushing me hard enough that I fell forward.

I hadn't even hit the ground yet when I saw my dad jump up and go after his belt. He hadn't seen the dog behind me.

"It wasn't me," I said, curled up in a ball on the ground. "Please! Misty pushed me. It wasn't my fault." I closed my eyes, tensing up in anticipation of the sting of the belt. My dad put the belt back through his belt loops. That time, I was spared.

That was unusual. My dad unleashed on me all the time for being a klutz, but I wasn't really clumsy. I was simply a little boy, who loved all kinds of sports and played hard. Falling was normal for a child. I never understood why it made him so mad. Even to this day, I don't really know why he beat me for it. Part of me thinks he used my falling or my mother's clothes as an excuse to vent his anger about work aggravations, money problems, one of Abuelo's personal criticisms—any one of a million other things that might have set him off.

But his rage was not just impersonal. He went berserk anytime he thought my mother or I had made him "look bad." He interpreted our actions as if we were out to embarrass him, even though they had nothing to do with him at all.

Yet, though he was so concerned about embarrassment, my dad didn't care if anyone witnessed him berating my mother or beating me into submission. One Thanksgiving dinner at my grandparents' house in Tijuana, I turned to my grandfather, who was seated next to me, and confided, "Abuelo, I've got to fart. It's hurting." I was eight years old at the time.

"You gotta fart, you gotta fart," he said. "Go ahead."

So I farted, and it was loud.

My dad looked up with an expression of sheer humiliation across his face, which quickly transformed into one of anger. The look my dad had in his eyes can only be described as that of a fucking terrorist. Always passionate about beating the hell out of me, he grabbed and pulled me into the other room. The rest of my family, including my guilt-ridden grandfather, listened helplessly to my wailing.

I was scared of my dad. So was my mom. His temper was how he got stuff done at work and at home. He could yell anyone into submission. When he really blew his top, he wasn't able to articulate anything. Instead, incomprehensible profanity streamed from his mouth. That's when you knew he was flipping his lid: he'd moved beyond words.

Ama and I never fought back. Unable to match his anger, we absorbed and internalized it. *We're wrong. This outfit is disgusting. I am a klutz who doesn't pay attention.* Mom and I wanted to get out from under his rule, but we were too scared. We discussed this explicitly from the time I was a young boy. Because we were too afraid to stand up to him, we simply obeyed.

We weren't the only ones who lived in fear of his short fuse. Among his business associates, his temper earned him the moniker "the Barker in Brioni." By the early '80s, he had a lot to bark about. Dad was feeling the financial squeeze.

Even with the fire chief and insurance claim adjuster in his pocket, he could only run the arson scam so many times before it became too obvious to get away with. By that time, though, he'd developed a relationship with the insurance man from one of the major insurance companies whose territory was the entire western seaboard from Canada to Mexico.

Together, my father and the insurance man cooked up a new scam: container insurance fraud. My dad would ship private containers to San Diego, Vancouver, or Tijuana. The containers would supposedly be filled with all kinds of expensive personal items, such as antiques or electronics. The insurance rep would then verify that the containers had landed with all the goods inside damaged, and my father would—thanks to his insurance policy—be compensated by the insurance company. But the containers of supposedly damaged goods were all, in reality, empty.

While my dad was a hothead with people, he was patient when it came to money, always choosing the longer, bigger con over smaller scams that greedier types would have taken more quickly. By the late '70s, he knew that there was no long-term future in insurance fraud. Meanwhile, he needed to figure out a way to maintain the upper-middle-class existence that my mother was accustomed to. This included sending me to my fancy private school, Francis W. Parker.

My mother had decided all the way back when she was in high school that when she had children, they would attend the prestigious K–12 private school in San Diego, and so she'd put me on a waiting list for kindergarten when I was only two weeks out of the womb. She herself had been the smartest girl at Our Lady of Peace, an all-girls Catholic school in San Diego, until ninth grade. That's when all the Tijuana elites who'd sent their daughters to Francis W. Parker transferred them out of the coed school and into Our Lady of Peace. By the time these girls reached high school, their conservative parents were more concerned with protecting their daughters' virginity than they were with promoting their education.

When the new girls arrived from Francis W. Parker, Ama noticed that they were a cut above. They were better mannered, smarter, better athletes, and more worldly—and my mom was no slouch. She was even accepted for admission at Stanford, which she'd applied to only to see if she could get in. She knew full well that she would never be able to attend. She was always going to follow what her culture and parents expected of her and get engaged by eighteen, then quickly marry and have kids. Still, the Francis W. Parker girls had left an indelible impression on her, and she never wavered from her conviction that I needed to attend that school, no matter what it cost my dad.

So my father needed more money. Other men might have turned to an influential father-in-law for help. My father did not. And Don Fernando stayed true to his promise and did not offer his son-in-law a job. In his whole lifetime, he never extended such an offer. He never forgave Jefe for embarrassing his family. According to my dad, my grandfather wouldn't support him in any way because he wanted to punish his son-in-law for getting his daughter pregnant out of wedlock.

I intuited this divide in our families from a very young age. From as early as I can remember, it was as if I lived in two different worlds. There was home in San Diego with Jefe and Ama. Then there was home with Abuelo and Abuela in Tijuana and on the ranch. But some invisible line separated these two homes from one another, just like the border we regularly breezed through that divided my two countries. My family was known to everyone at the American and Mexican customs gates, and we were allowed to circumvent the hundreds of cars and trucks lined up on both sides of the crossing.

Somehow, in my young mind, my parents and grandparents were so separate that for a time, I didn't even realize they were related. One day when I was four, an age at which most kids have a firm grasp on the relationship between their grandparents and their parents, I asked Ama, "Mom, those people you send me to every weekend, who are they?"

She was driving but looked at me in the back seat of the car through the rearview mirror. "Well, you know how I'm your ama?" she said.

I nodded in the affirmative.

"Well, Abuelo and Abuela are my mommy and daddy."

In families, the unspoken can be as loud, if not louder, than the spoken. Now that my question had been answered, I somehow knew not to bring up the subject of my grandparents around my father and vice versa. I was following my mother's example; the mention of any relationship to her parents in front of her husband was tantamount to betrayal.

The divide was about more than Abuelo holding a grudge against my dad for knocking up my mom. The two men were also like night and day. Though my father was two decades older than my mother, he was only ten years younger than his father-in-law. And yet he and my grandfather had opposite personalities, moralities, and lifestyles.

My dad was an entrepreneur and a con man, the only difference between the identities being the legality of the enterprise—and sometimes the area in between the two was quite gray. For my dad, the only question he had about a moneymaking idea was, "Can you go to jail for it?" If the answer was "Very unlikely," then he was in—even if the prospect did involve breaking laws.

My grandfather, on the other hand, was never on the wrong side of the law—or at least, not in a way that wasn't culturally acceptable. Falsifying Mexican government documents to speed up the process, smuggling in a cheetah for a professional associate's private zoo, and paying bribes regularly were not viewed as incidents of lawbreaking. These activities were simply the price of doing business.

Since inheriting the customshouse brokerage firm, Abuelo had built a solid business into a vast empire—not through scams but by keeping his nose to the grindstone. At the height of his success, he had three hundred employees. But no matter how many people worked for him, Don Fernando was always the first one to arrive at work. He was the consummate patriarch, a respectable man who stressed the importance of family and never lost his cool. He was quiet when it came to his anger. It was his silence that broke people. Like I said, the opposite of my dad.

The enmity between the two men explained why my father didn't have any fun at the ranch. He's the only person I ever knew who didn't. My father did not fit in there, because the ranch was 100 percent my abuelo's. While everyone was coming in from the day's ride—their boots and gear dirty after a long, exhilarating adventure, laughing and patting one another on the backs as they grabbed ice-cold bottles of Pacifico—there sat my dad, nursing a snifter of Grand Marnier.

Even Jefe's drink was out of place. He chose it in part because he actually hated alcohol. He viewed drunkenness as a weakness, pure and simple. But he also knew that in Mexico, drinking was a social norm. As Abuelo used to say: "I need to drink with you to trust you." And so, while my grandfather got sloppy wasted—grabbing men by the shoulders and singing loudly to mariachi music—my dad glowered over the syrupy orange liqueur in his glass. He could tolerate only sweet alcohol, like Grand Marnier or Lancers wine. Even then, he would take only a few sips and dump the rest on the ground. He would have given anything to swap it for his favorite drink on earth, Coca-Cola.

My family was split, culturally, financially, temperamentally. On one side was my family in Mexico, who thought my father was an awful guy who couldn't be trusted. Back in San Diego, my dad had equally unpleasant things to say about them. And me? I was always in the middle. I loved my abuelo and felt at peace on the ranch. But my dad was, well, my dad. Someone I had to love but I didn't like.

By the time I was almost twelve, however, I had begun to think of my grandfather as a father figure more than I did my actual dad. This was partly because I spent more time with him than I did with my dad. Even though I was home all week, I hardly saw my father, who didn't come home every night until late. And even when I did see him, he was usually in a foul mood. At the ranch, I stayed by my grandfather's side almost the entire time. He took pleasure in showing me everything, from how to ride to how to treat staff and greet guests. He taught me everything.

I grew so attached to my abuelo that eventually I didn't even want to come home on Sundays. Since my grandfather woke so early to go to work, it was easy enough for him to drop me home Monday mornings before school. By 1980, the arrangement had evolved to the point that I was spending Friday through Monday with my grandparents.

As far as I was concerned, the less I saw my father, the better. That was particularly true in 1982 when the Mexican government devalued the peso in response to a mounting debt crisis. At that time, a global recession had brought about a significant loss in revenue from the country's oil exports. The currency devaluation had been the response to the ensuing financial crisis. Mexicans had anxiously watched their currency go from 25 to 150 pesos per dollar seemingly overnight. And the forecast predicted a continued decline.

I was too young then to really understand what was going on. But I remember the nightly newscasts that showed cars flooding the border with people looking to exchange their increasingly worthless pesos for dollars. Even more memorable to me are the faces of my family members, which looked worried.

Everyone in the country was struggling to some degree. That included us. Many others were struggling more. But that fact didn't make my parents and grandparents worry any less. Dad was definitely in a precarious position. After he had taken insurance fraud as far as it could go, he'd developed a relationship with the governor of a particular

Mexican state and gotten involved in a garden-variety political-corruption scam that was rampant at the time.

The scam involved skimming off government contracts. The process was simple: Government bureaucrats involved in the scam would give the governor half a million dollars to build a greenhouse, which only costs $50,000 to construct. After the $50,000 was paid out, everyone involved would split the profits. This included the bureaucrat who'd awarded the contract, the construction company, and my dad: the middleman who put the whole scam together.

Word had gotten around that my dad knew how to take a little money off the top of government deals—a lot of money, actually. The first governor had sent him on to elected officials in other regions, which was how my father started to develop a rapport with the country's most corrupt politicians—of which there were many.

Once the Mexican economy tanked, however, the government contracts had all dried up. There was no infrastructure being built because there was no money available for building. During the peso's dramatic collapse, people lost upward of 80 percent of their wealth in about a month. Everyone was panicking, including my dad. Instead of smoking one pack of cigarettes a day, he was now smoking two.

Because of this state of affairs, I was surprised when Dad announced that after the first big devaluation of 1982, we were going on vacation, and not just anywhere but to Cancún. In the early '80s, Cancún was the "it" place to go. Wealthy Mexicans had abandoned Acapulco, which had become too developed to be considered exclusive. Now they traveled to the unspoiled white-sand beaches of Cancún. But I wasn't one to question my father.

We stayed at the Grand Park Royal Cancún, which had two pools right off a majestic beach, where my dad lay out in his Speedo each day, all day, much to my embarrassment. (He loved his tiny fucking European bathing suits until his dying day.)

We didn't go on vacation alone. The governor who had been skimming off contracts with my dad was also there with his family. So while my mom and the governor's wife played backgammon poolside, and while his kids and I played in the surf, the two men discussed their future—which, in my dad's case, did not look good. With the Mexican currency devaluation having gone upward of 50 percent, and with oil revenue growth looking anemic, the country was facing down the possibility of stratospheric inflation rates as President José López Portillo finished up his six-year term. The successor to Mexico's longtime ruling Institutional Revolutionary Party and Portillo's budget and planning minister, Miguel de la Madrid, was a conservative technocrat who'd been anointed to bring order to the economic chaos. De la Madrid had vowed to Mexicans, who were sick of the corruption that ran through every aspect of their country, that he would push "a more egalitarian society" and "moral renovation."

That did not bode well for middlemen like my dad whose stock-in-trade was corruption.

"Pietro, I don't know what you are going to do," the now-former governor told him. The vacation was a cover for the men to meet without suspicion. The ex-governor had transitioned into the field of education. He didn't want to do anything that might risk his new position as the *secretaría de educación pública*, Mexico's national education ministry. "I can't help you at all," he said. "Everything's gone. All the money, the connections. Gone."

They say necessity is the mother of invention. In my father's case, it was a case of misery being the mother of profit. "Picho, where there is devastation," he once told me, "there is opportunity."

He had his epiphany while on the beach—in that goddamn Speedo. For months we'd been watching news stories on TV about desperate Mexicans who were crossing the border in order to change their unstable currency for the most stable currency in the world, the American dollar. They could only do this at foreign exchanges abroad.

At that time, the dollar was king across the planet. American currency was accepted in any country in the world. But in Mexico, *everyone* wanted to be paid dollars if possible. The dollar was worth way more than the peso, which seemed to be worth less with every passing day. Because everyone was trying to get to the American money exchanges, it took a long time for the average Mexican citizen to cross over to the US side. It could take as long as four hours for pedestrian traffic to cross the San Ysidro border. This was a real impediment for those who wanted to turn pesos into dollars as fast as they could.

For the last day and a half of the trip, my typically voluble father went radio silent. You could also see it in his eyes: he was cooking something up. It wasn't until we were on the flight home that he announced his plan. That's when my dad turned to my mom and said the words that would change so much for us.

"I'm going to start a foreign exchange."

CHAPTER 4

PE$OS

For the next three to four days after arriving home from Cancún, I didn't see my dad. And for once, it wasn't because he was out at Matteottis with his boys. Instead, he'd sequestered himself in his office at home, where he was working out the details on his plan to open a foreign exchange. When my dad was focused on something he wanted, he was all in. When he came out of his office for meals, we could see the concentration on his face. Even as he ate dinner with us, my mom and I could tell he wasn't really there.

Opening and operating a foreign exchange would provide an opportunity for him to return to legitimate business, a path that he'd abandoned the day he burned down Portofino. Exchanges, where customers change one currency for another, make money by charging fees on each transaction, usually in the form of a percentage of the exchange rate.

For example, if an exchange rate were a perfect 1 to 1, the person exchanging money would not get a full dollar back. They might get 98 or 97 percent back. The exchange operation—that is, the middleman responsible for exchanging the two currencies—pockets the difference. So the exchange operation my father proposed was a legal enterprise.

But this wasn't why he wanted to do it. Jefe was an entrepreneur without a conscience. He looked at all opportunities, illegal or not, the same way. The question was always: Is there money to be made?

He had his work cut out for him. Because of his lack of resources, he had to create the exchange on a shoestring. He found an empty parking lot in the San Ysidro neighborhood of San Diego right on the US-Mexico border. Known as the Gateway to the Americas, San Ysidro is the busiest border crossing in the world. Dad made a deal with the owner to rent the parking lot and then brought two shipping containers to the bare-bones property. He then strung them together, cut out a little window and door, and turned the containers into an office.

My mom and I were not impressed when he took us to see his finished project: PL Money Exchange.

"This is it?" my mom said as she looked around the building. It was kind of janky, definitely compared to Portofino, the fine-clothing store. The containers were only temporary, Jefe explained: a necessary, if unsightly, short-term solution. This operation was going to be big, he assured us.

That was about the extent of the questions my mother ever asked about my dad's work. He generally didn't discuss the details of his business life with her, and she was fine with that. After he'd closed down Portofino and gotten involved in insurance fraud, he told her that he was in "construction." That explanation was good enough for her. Theirs was a marriage based on traditional roles: my dad paid the bills, and my mother dealt with the domestic side of life. I was the center of her universe, and she was more than happy to tune out the rest.

The rest, at this point in time, meant Jefe's money exchange. If the new endeavor didn't work out, it wouldn't be for lack of trying. He had a different attitude now than he'd had in his prior work. He was going to be dealing with currency in the US. That meant he had to keep things on the up-and-up, as well as consider and attend to every detail. Jefe naively believed that, in contrast to Mexico's anything-goes attitude, legitimate American business ran on the straight and narrow. It wouldn't take long, however, for him to realize that criminals are everywhere.

Once he'd hung his shingle of his "office," Mom and I hardly ever saw my dad. When I woke up in the morning for school, I would find him sleeping on the couch because he had come in late and didn't want to disturb my mother. We absolutely lost Dad whenever he got obsessed with work. This was fine with my mom and me because when he was occupied, he didn't have the energy or the time to berate us or beat up on us.

He was definitely putting in the hours. Opening up early and staying open until very late, he was burning the candle at both ends. So it was a strange staffing move when he brought my uncle on board. Fernando Gutierrez Jr. was a man who was known for a lot of things, but none of them was hard work.

With his long curly hair and equally flamboyant personality, Nando was the ultimate Latin playboy. If he had any ambition at all, it lay in the pursuit of hot women, fast cars, fun parties, and nice things. Money was the route to them all, but he had zero interest in holding down an honest job. He preferred an easy payday, like the time when my parents were still dating and my dad bribed Nando—who was my mom's little brother and their official chaperone—to look the other way while he and my mom made out.

My uncle's fuzzy sense of morality might have had something to do with being raised to believe he could do no wrong. In a way, his upbringing was not all that different from that of my father, who as the treasured son in a family of girls had also been made to feel like he was the center of the universe. Their narcissism was one of many shared traits that would bond the two men, for better or worse.

Nando was born nine years after my mom, and the news of his arrival came as such a surprise, my grandfather thought at first that it was a prank. Before she got pregnant with Nando, my grandmother had suffered multiple miscarriages. She was thrilled to finally carry another pregnancy to term and beyond overjoyed when she delivered a baby—on April Fools' Day. My grandfather was out that night when the waiter at the restaurant he was at brought the landline with the extra-long cord to his table: "Fernando, your wife's going into labor." Abuelo thought they were pulling his leg, because he rarely went out for the evening. Later on, he got another call. This time, it was the doctor: "Don Fernando, you have a boy."

The cherished prince had arrived. Nando was my grandmother's pride and joy. He was proof that she had attained the most important goal of any wife: to provide her husband with a son. Even long after Nando proved he was not fit to take over the customshouse from Abuelo, he remained the center of my grandmother's universe. She adored him more than she did anyone else on the planet: more than her husband, more than her daughter.

That alone would have been enough to explain my mother's conflicted feelings about Nando. But there was more to it than that. Her brother had also usurped her role in the family simply by virtue of his gender. After my grandmother's many miscarriages, my grandfather had for a time assumed that they wouldn't have any more children. Since he did not have a son, he raised my mom to be the one who would protect his fortune and maybe even take over the business. That meant raising her, for the first nine years of her life, like a boy.

When he took her riding on the weekends, she mimicked him in every way, right down to the boots. At the ranch in Rosarito, there hung a large portrait of my grandfather and mother, sitting atop horses. In the painting, they have the exact same posture: straight-backed, one hand on a hip, like a pair of French generals. If a person missed the ponytail, they could easily have mistaken my mother for a boy. Both wore the same stern expression on their faces. It was impossible to miss the resemblance.

Then my uncle came along and everything changed. My mom had been raised to believe she would run the show one day. Now, suddenly, she was the girl who would eventually be married off. At nine, well after her childhood identity had been formed, she was forced into an entirely different role from the one she'd initially been given.

As adults, the brother and sister loved each other very much. But it was also obvious that there was always an underlying jealousy. She never forgave Nando for taking over as heir apparent. Thanks to my uncle's birth, my mom had lost much of the respect and centrality she had once earned in her family. At the same time, she was proud to have fulfilled the role of wife and mother that was expected of her.

My grandmother coddled Nando—and so, to some extent, did my grandfather. The fact that my mother harbored resentment against her baby brother didn't keep her from coddling him too. By the time he reached adulthood, he wasn't equipped to do anything for himself: whether that meant saddling his own horse or getting a college degree. It wasn't really his fault. Nando didn't know how to do any of those things since, from the moment he was born, he had been handed everything he wanted on a silver platter.

First, Don Fernando bribed his son's way into Anáhuac University in Mexico City and then had to pay someone to write Nando's papers. Eventually, he had to make another donation in order for Nando to graduate two years late with a degree in law. Nando wasn't really a lawyer, because he didn't know anything about the law. But he got the title, which he wanted, because his dad paid for it. My uncle certainly never intended to practice law. He was content with living in his sweet condo in Mexico City after graduation and doing not much of anything.

Don Fernando, however, was not content with that arrangement, and at a certain point, he put his foot down: Nando must return home, he said. And Nando did. Although he spent most of his time at the ranch, where he could get out from under the disapproving gaze of his hardworking father. Nando would come out for the weekend with a group of his friends and then stay there with them after the rest of us had returned to the city for work and school. He and his friends would lie out around the pool or go riding during the day and party at Rosarito's small bar scene into the wee hours of the morning.

Every woman he met thought he was very attractive, even though he wasn't all that good-looking. He didn't have traditionally handsome features. But somehow the funky nose and long, curly black hair worked in harmony with his suave demeanor to create a whole cohesive package. Many years later, after I was grown up and married, my wife, Michelle, met a nice woman through mutual charity work. It turned out that she had visited the ranch as a girl because her father was Abuelo's physician. Though probably forty years had passed, the woman lit up like a swooning celebrity fan describing Nando. "When he rode up on a horse with white pants and shirt," she said, "my jaw dropped. He was the sexiest man I had ever seen."

Nando, whom I called Tio Fer, always made an impression. He was cool and a ton of fun. He would stay up all night and continue the party into the next day. At some point in the '70s, my uncle even turned one of the three bedrooms at the ranch into a disco, complete with a disco ball and a small dance floor made of fake white marble surrounded by shag carpet and pillows—a poor man's version of the Playboy mansion. There were no discos in Rosarito, so my uncle would ask women he met at the bars if they wanted to go dancing. If their answer was yes, he said, "Come back to my house? I have a disco at my ranch." More times than not, the line worked.

Tio would stay up for two or three days until he finally came crashing down and slept for twenty-four hours straight. Once, after reviving himself from one of his benders, Tio Fer told me that his ability to stay awake for days and party so heroically was rooted in a medical condition.

"The doctors say I have some type of interesting blood that gives me all the energy in the world," he said. Today, I know what his *special energy* was; it was called *blow*. I realized this only years later, after I had done cocaine myself. *That* had been the source of his energy. But when I was a kid, I believed every word he said.

My uncle had an indestructible quality, like the kind demonstrated by rock stars. At the very least, he was the rock star of our family. Nothing could take him down. It didn't matter how much he drank or how many drugs he did, how many women he slept with or how fast he drove. And Nando drove *fast*. He had a hot car, a Datsun 280Z, that he drove so fast that in one completely drunken moment, he went right off a bridge. He didn't actually fly off the middle of the bridge in Rosarito, like some scene from an action movie. He simply careened off the abutment. Still, his car fell nose-first ten feet from the ground! He should have been killed; instead, he walked away unharmed.

I looked up to Tio Fer, whom I thought of as more of a big brother than an uncle. Thirteen years my senior, he included me in as many activities as possible. I wanted to be just like him, and I knew he would do anything for me. One time when I was five years old, Abuelo had decided to bring a bull to the ranch so he could host a bullfight. During a break in the event, I decided to jump into the ring with the bull. As soon as he noticed, my uncle jumped the fence without hesitating, ran, and grabbed me as the bull started to charge in my direction. He threw me over the fence and then quickly followed, before the bull reached us. The bull probably wasn't the biggest and fiercest or as close on our heels as it felt. But the worry—and love—etched on my uncle's face is something I'll never forget.

Abuelo didn't quite view his son as the hero I did. Don Fernando had indeed gotten a son at last. But with every wild party and every refusal to join the family brokerage, it became clearer to my grandfather that Nando was not a son who would follow in his father's footsteps. My grandmother was the great enabler, making any and every excuse why Nando shouldn't work at the customshouse. "He's got a different head on his shoulders." "Let him do his own thing." "Give it a little more time." She was the excuse factory. Considering how it all turned out, she should have insisted her son go to work for his father. She didn't have that in her, though, maybe because she understood on some level that my uncle didn't have the capacity to handle the job.

My grandmother tried to shield my grandfather from seeing Nando's inadequacies. She wanted to make sure that her husband saw her son in the best light possible. This sometimes caused her to behave in surprising ways. For example, Abuela usually waited for my grandfather to open the passenger door for her before she ever got out of the car. But not when we arrived at the ranch on Sunday mornings. Then decorum fell by the wayside.

On those mornings, she was always the first one out of the car and into the house, because she wanted to clean up any disasters Nando had created the night before. "What's wrong?" she always asked the staff before quickly devising a plan to keep whatever it was from my grandfather. If there was a mess in a certain part of the house, Robert would be summoned to take Abuelo out to attend to some "important" matter that concerned the horses.

Then, before storming into Nando's room, she would ask the staff, "How many girls are in there?" She yelled at the hookers to get out and told girls she knew to put their clothes on "before I have to say something to your mother." Her full-service damage-control efforts on Sunday mornings were all part of the cover-up that Abuelo allowed. He wasn't stupid. Each of them played their part, as family members tend to do when trying to dance around disappointment. But despite all this, Abuelo still could not hide the bitter disapproval he felt when Nando decided to go into business with my dad.

Ever since the days when my uncle had chaperoned my parents, he and my dad had gotten to know each other, and they'd grown fond of one another. Nando appreciated the very same things about the cool Italian guy dating his sister that his father hated, right down to the flashy suits and the funny accent. Nando and my father also bonded over the fact that both chafed under Don Fernando's rules. In that sense, it wasn't surprising when my dad approached my uncle about joining in on the foreign exchange. "You don't have to do much," Dad promised. Those were the magic words. My uncle didn't hesitate.

Unlike her father, Ama loved the fact that her brother and her husband had gone into business together. She eventually helped her father see things her way. "At least he's working," she said, "and not just at the ranch partying." Abuelo had to agree that it was nice for Nando to be making his own money for a change. Because of this, my grandfather and father's contentious relationship eased up during this time as much as it ever would. Our family never got along better than it did at the start of the money exchange.

My father, however, had not hired Nando out of the goodness of his heart. He was a con man who'd lured my uncle into the business on the basis of their relationship. In truth, he just needed an American citizen who could open up bank accounts on the US side of the border with ease.

Jefe hadn't been wrong in believing that the money exchange would be lucrative. He quickly had more business than he could handle. In the beginning, the transactions were manageable. But it didn't take long for word to get out about a new player in the exchange market. There was so much demand that, although Jefe crammed as many people as he could into the makeshift shipping-container office, the wait to get into PL Exchange could sometimes be four blocks long. Even worse, he sometimes had to close his doors—even as early as the middle of the day—because he'd run out of dollars.

The only time PL Exchange wasn't open was when Jefe ran out of dollars. That was the commodity that made the business run. He exchanged dollars for pesos to the customers at a certain rate, then brought the pesos to the bank to sell them back at a better rate than he'd bought them for. Margins were tight. It was the quantity and constancy of the money exchanged that fueled the real profit. It was a daily race to offload the bad currency as fast as possible, because pesos were a liability.

Then he was off hunting for more dollars. He was always trying to get more dollars. He was either calling banks in the US or, more often than not, making quick visits to eight, nine different banks, trying to restock his supply. But so were owners of all the other exchanges. When he couldn't find the dollars he needed, he had no other choice but to close up for the day.

It was easy for Ama and me to tell when Jefe had run out of dollars, because then he was home. The amount of time we saw him was inversely proportional to the success of his business in those early days. He went deep into the effort, working as much as he could. For the first five months, we rarely saw him. On the days he ran out of dollars, however, he had nothing to do. I'd return home from school and find him on the couch.

His presence wasn't a cause for celebration, because the fact that he was home also meant he was going to be in a foul mood. Money drove his temper. Ama and I wanted him working, because when he was home with us, he wasn't a reassuring fatherly figure. He was a dick. My father was now smoking five or six packs a day. The pressure to keep up with the demand for dollars was intense. But Jefe was going to get them, one way or another.

CHAPTER 5

TOUCHING TEN MILLION

Jefe couldn't get out of those shipping containers fast enough. He worked night and day, exchanging pesos as they continued their downward slide and hustling for the dollars needed for the transactions. By the fall of 1983, less than four months after he got into the trade, he'd made enough money to rent a storefront right next to the parking lot and move his exchange there. He was also able to open a second exchange in a little kiosk so close to the border that people could walk across to it.

His success exacerbated the central problem with his business: insufficient access to dollars. He couldn't keep up with demand from the Mexicans who poured across the border to exchange their money. He was buying dollars from local San Diego banks, but these small branches and independent financial institutions just didn't have enough supply. He realized that in order to get more product, he would need to make the jump to bigger banks. This conviction was further reinforced when someone at the Coronado branch of a national US bank told him that in order to get the kind of cash he was talking about, he needed to speak to someone at the bank's California headquarters in San Francisco.

Fueled by the same drive that had gotten him out of those containers, Jefe called until he reached someone at the office of foreign currency at the bank and convinced the guy to talk to his boss about the overheated PL Exchange on the Tijuana border. When the man's boss agreed to a meeting, my dad said he could be in San Francisco as early as the day after next. The meeting could easily be held over the phone, the bank employee told him.

"No, I want to meet in person," Jefe said.

If my father was good at anything, it was making connections. He must have known that he would make a bigger impression on Federico Ricci—the head of the currency division at the national bank in San Francisco and another Italian—if they saw each other in the flesh. And he was right.

The two old-school Italians, both seeking their fortunes on the West Coast of the United States, felt an instant camaraderie. Ricci liked my dad, or at least spoke his native language. But he didn't know much about Jefe's business.

Since Ricci managed the foreign-exchange desk, he was naturally aware of the devalued peso. But he didn't know about the micro industry that had cropped up along the border. He hadn't heard that wealthy Mexicans had to make many trips over the border to exchange their pesos in amounts under the $10,000 taxable limit. These tax laws meant my father's clients were repeat customers by necessity.

As Jefe explained what was happening, Ricci grew more and more interested. Finally, he decided that the business opportunity was big enough to warrant making a trip down to the border himself. Just as my dad had insisted on meeting in person, the bank exec needed to see with his own eyes the day-to-day operations of this foreign-exchange frenzy.

When Ricci visited San Ysidro on a three-day trip to witness my father's operation along the border, he was bowled over by the traffic he saw coming through PL Exchange. "Is it like this every day?" he asked.

"As long as the peso still continues to devalue," my dad said.

His eyes wide with excitement, Ricci said, "You know, Pietro, I think this is going to make sense." Now that the offer was on the table, it was time to get into the details. "How much do you need?" he asked my dad.

Jefe needed to borrow around $20 million every month to run the operation. Seeing more than a hint of enthusiasm on Ricci's face, Jefe decided to reach for the stars and ask for $30 million. It was a negotiation tactic to give himself enough wiggle room to land at his lower, and real, number.

When he asked for the $30 million a month loan, Ricci just laughed.

Oh, fuck, thought my dad, as he later told it to my mom and me. *I asked for too much money, and now this guy's laughing at me like I'm crazy or stupid.*

But that wasn't at all why Ricci was laughing.

"You don't need thirty million," Ricci told my father. "You need *a hundred* million."

He explained that my dad needed to expand, open more locations across the border, in order to capitalize on the great business opportunity he had been smart enough to discover. Jefe's goal, Ricci said, should be to get bigger—and that was a proposition that would take serious money.

When my dad came home from that meeting, he was on fire. He had just secured a deal with a major US bank to get a line of credit of $100 million! His days of scrounging for dollars were over now that he had access to more than he would ever need. Which, even someone as greedy as my dad had to admit, seemed strange.

It didn't make sense to him that Ricci had offered him more money than he could use. "I don't need it," my dad told us. "I don't care what he says. Even if I open three, four locations, that won't cost me *that* much money." Bankers, conservative by nature, were not known to throw around cash. So my dad wasn't just surprised and pleased by the development, he was also a little skeptical.

His grifter sense was twitching. As imposing a person as my dad could appear to be, he was still a small fish when compared to someone like Ricci, who ran an entire division of a major bank. My dad was a hustler. Ricci was corporate. The latter had all the power over the former, and my dad knew it.

But he wasn't going to let something as little as a deal that didn't quite add up ruin the experience of $100 million at his disposal. "I don't need it," he said with his characteristic bravado. "But if that changes, then great. I will use it."

Not long after he settled the deal with the bank, my dad told me, "I'm bringing you to the exchange today. I want you to see something."

The only time Jefe brought my mother or me to work was when he wanted to brag. He'd brought us to the shipping container that marked the opening of PL Money Exchange. He'd trotted us out again when he expanded the exchange to a brick-and-mortar store and kiosk. The premise of these field trips was that they were for our benefit. They were a glimpse into, and an education about, his very important work. But Jefe's tours were always polluted by an unappealing undercurrent of neediness, as if their real purpose was to win our approval. He reminded me of an insecure kid who thinks he can make friends by showing off his expensive new toys.

Now, the first month's massive loan from Ricci was being delivered to his office, and he wanted my mom and me to see it in person.

Thirty million dollars.

Five safes full of money.

In my dad's little office on the border.

His plan worked. My mom and I were more than impressed. We were in shock.

Never one to miss an opportunity, Jefe must have read amazement on my face, because he decided to take the show one step further.

"Picho, come," he said while we stood in the vault that held the safes.

He beckoned me over to a briefcase. When I was standing by his side, he popped the briefcase open, and there inside were many perfect piles of hundred-dollar bills.

"Touch it," my dad said.

I put my hand out and skimmed the stacks with my fingers, the rough, dry paper of cash powdery to the touch.

"You are touching one million dollars."

That was cool. And scary. Especially for my dad, apparently, because the week Ricci delivered the money, he refused to leave his office, even to go to sleep. He couldn't keep his eyes off the money. Literally. The vault could only be accessed through a door in his office, which was behind his desk, over Jefe's left shoulder. The singular point of entry to all that money was through his desk, through him. So my dad slept in his chair, his feet up on his big desk in between two massive crystal ashtrays, his landline, and a brick-size 1980s cell phone. It made sense that he wanted to monitor the vault during the day, just in case any employees decided to pocket some cash. Sleeping there, however, was more about his ego and need for control than anything else. He wasn't even armed. Still, if someone was going to walk in and try to take his money, they would have to get through him first.

He probably would have slept there permanently if Ama hadn't finally put her foot down. After he'd slept in his office for three nights in a row, my mother drove over to the exchange and yanked him out. "You need to sleep," she said.

"I've slept," he said. "I'm sleeping here."

"No, you need to sleep in your own fucking bed."

Then, in early 1984, months after Ricci's trip to the border, my father found out the real reason a major bank wanted to lend a small exchange in San Ysidro way more money than it needed. The truth came out after Jefe got a strange, unannounced walk-up meeting request from representatives of the Dunes Hotel and Casino.

The Dunes had been one of the original resorts on the Strip when it opened in 1955. The first sight people arriving in Las Vegas from Southern California encountered was the sprawling hotel-casino that was nicknamed "The Miracle in the Desert" and the "Diamond of the Dunes." For a time, the twenty-four-story hotel tower, bringing the resort up to 450 rooms, was the tallest building in Nevada. By the '80s, the Dunes had ballooned to a mammoth operation with 1,300 rooms, two swimming pools that offered poolside gaming, a dry-cleaning plant, an eighteen-hole championship golf course that was the largest in the state, and an arena that held major professional boxing matches for more than a decade.

Despite all its bells and whistles, however, the Dunes struggled to stay afloat. In 1984, it filed for bankruptcy protection with $184 million in obligations and losses of $30 million from the previous year. Over its three decades, the Dunes had had a succession of owners. Some of them had had ties to the mob, and others had, themselves, been mobsters.

At the time of the Chapter 11 protection filing, the casino's operator was Morris Shenker, whom *Life* magazine dubbed the "foremost lawyer for the mob in the US." Shenker had been an attorney for Jimmy Hoffa, the president of the International Brotherhood of Teamsters. The teamsters union, famously affiliated with the mob, had made him the loan that allowed him to purchase the controlling interest in the Dunes. Although he was never charged with any crime, officials had certainly tried to build a case against him. Shenker was formally investigated by the FBI, SEC, IRS, and other government agencies.

Jefe agreed to meet with the Dunes representatives when it quickly became apparent he had no other choice. Given the background of the Dunes's owner, perhaps it wasn't totally surprising that these men spoke to my father in his native tongue, since Italian was the language spoken by many members of the mafia.

But everything they said to him came as a great surprise.

"We have been made aware that you have an extra seventy million at your disposal," one of the reps said to him. "And we would like you to loan us your extra cash to cover the outstanding chips on the casino floor on weekends."

A person didn't have to be a rocket scientist to figure out how this information had gotten to the Dunes. All of a sudden, it made perfect sense why Ricci had been so eager to lend my father $100 million, and Jefe understood perfectly that Ricci hadn't done it out of the kindness of his heart or out of his belief in my dad's business acumen.

In the '80s, Las Vegas was undergoing a transition. Previously, it had been controlled by crime syndicates. Now, it was increasingly falling under corporate control.

Mafia families and their associates, who'd built the original casinos and hotels, had maintained a grip on the Strip until the late '70s, when government regulators began to take a heavy hand. The Nevada Gaming Control Board continued to crack down on illegal practices. An even more powerful force of change, however, was the Wall Street money that had started to find its way to the casino floors. Whereas the mob could cough up $20 million at once, financier Michael Milken's junk bonds were able to spit out $600 million to invest in a resort. And we have a winner! By the '90s, Milken and casino executive Steve Wynn had turned Vegas into a place that was safe for both families and investment funds.

At the point when the Dunes reps approached my dad, however, conservative financial institutions like the major US bank Ricci worked for weren't supposed to do business with casinos. Still tainted by its mafioso reputation, Las Vegas was frowned upon by the banks, by the government, and in the court of public opinion.

The reason Ricci was so excited to have my dad as his client was that he had found a pawn he could use to loan $70 million to the Dunes Hotel and Casino while still keeping his bank's hands clean. My dad was the perfect mark for several reasons. He had no other source for the $30 million he needed every month to keep his business running. The exchange—where the money would go—was located along the Tijuana border, where Jefe could easily keep people from asking too many questions about trucks carrying big loads of cash. And lastly, Jefe was a fellow Italian, who spoke the same language as Ricci and the guys from the Dunes.

When he learned the truth, my dad felt like a fool. Sitting in our living room when he returned from San Francisco, he shook his head and said, *"Me vieron la cara de pendejo."*

The saying, commonly used in Mexico, has many meanings. "Don't look at me like I have a stupid face" is sometimes used as a cautionary statement meant to convey confidence and warn the other party that you are standing your ground. But its main purpose is to convey that a person feels stupid—and not a benign kind of stupid. It means that someone *made* you feel stupid—because you *were* stupid—and now you want to kick his ass for it.

That was the depth of my father's bitterness when he told my mom and me what had happened. Landing a big and smart deal with a major bank had made him feel like he was the man. But Ricci had just been using him to facilitate his own secret deal.

"They made me look like a fucking idiot," Dad said. There was nothing he hated more than being reminded of the limits of his power—nothing, that is, except losing money.

My father looked at the situation in three, then five, then ten different ways. But there was nothing to be done about it. He had no choice but to give the fuckers the money. Ricci had gotten him good. He was pissed as hell that the banker had manipulated him into a corner. At the same time, my dad admired Ricci for it. The truth was, if he'd had the connections, position, and smarts to pull off something like that himself, he would have done the exact same thing.

Jefe had been played, for sure. But the situation wasn't all bad for my dad. Not only did he get to keep his $30 million to use, the proposition from the Dunes reps was pretty good too.

"You'll collect a nice vig," one of the men from the Dunes said. He loosely used the term for the fee bookies charge when they place a bet to signify the little extra my dad would get for his troubles. "And when this type of loan brings you higher-profile clients, which it definitely will, our facilities are at your convenience for them—or you."

In fact, once my father's wounded pride had healed, he actually grew excited about the prospect of having a mutually beneficial relationship with the casino. Jefe wasn't the first man—and wouldn't be the last—to be seduced by the allure of Vegas. He rationalized that the lucrative arrangement was beneficial for everyone. The money was coming from the bank and going to a place where the house always wins. He was just the middleman. *What could possibly go wrong?* he thought.

"No harm, no foul," he declared to the guy from the Dunes. "You got it. Let's go ahead."

Jefe, the Dunes, and Ricci agreed upon a deal that transformed PL Exchange from a completely legit business to a less-legit one. And that's how two Brinks trucks from the bank came to roll up to the back door of my father's foreign exchange one Thursday afternoon in the spring of '84, well in time for the weekend—like it did every month as part of a revolving loan. The entire security team my dad employed—all ex–Navy SEALs and US military men—was waiting for the bank's first delivery of the full amount of the loan to the PL Exchange. Most of the cash would be going directly on to Las Vegas. The blond-haired, blue-eyed studs were strategically positioned in what looked like a tactical formation learned during their armed-forces training. One guy was on the roof surveying the area; the rest surrounded the exchange building. All were armed to the teeth.

My dad had hired the security guards not long after he made the deal with Ricci and the Dunes, and they were always packing. This was a time when Mexico was plagued with kidnappings. People even believed that kidnappers had associates who were working inside banks, because they usually set ransom demands at the exact amount of money a person held in their account. Ransoms had become the price of doing business in Mexico, so much so that many foreign executives took out insurance to cover them in the event that they were abducted. Jefe knew a target had been put on all our backs the moment he started to trade in a lot of money, so he got guards for my mother and me as well.

My personal security guard, Alex—also ex-military—carried no fewer than three guns on him when he drove me to and from school. He wore one on his ankle, one in a side holster, and one strapped to his back. An eighth-grade boy, I was fascinated by Alex's badass ways. I was constantly asking him questions about his guns and military exploits. One day, after I'd noticed that he sometimes sped up and slowed down for no apparent reason during our drives to school, I asked him what he was doing.

"Never have a car on both sides of you," he said. "You always need an exit."

That was the reason why he rarely drove in the two middle lanes. Alex's rule has always stuck with me. To this day, I will speed up or slow down whenever cars are directly to my right and left.

In the money drop at Jefe's exchange, the Brinks guards poured out of the vehicles—one truck carrying the full $100 million and the other one empty. They surrounded the trucks, their sunglasses and weapons glinting in the Southern California sun. They unloaded $30 million from one truck and deposited it into my dad's foreign exchange, and the other $70 million was loaded into the empty truck. The entire operation took no more than three minutes.

Then the Brinks guys jumped back into the trucks. The empty vehicle returned to the secure parking facility at Brinks headquarters, and the one filled with cash sped off to the airport, where a plane waited to carry it directly to the Dunes.

CHAPTER 6

KING OF THE PESO

The plane door opened onto another cloudless, eighty-five-degree day in Las Vegas. After sitting for an hour in refrigerated cabin air, the dry heat felt good to me as Jefe, my best friend Will Beamer, and I filed down the ramp stairs to the tarmac along with the rest of the passengers. Unlike the other fliers, though, who turned right for the short walk to the airport terminal, we took a left and walked to where a limo, sent courtesy of the Dunes Hotel and Casino, sat idling, waiting for us.

Planeside pickup was just the first in a seemingly endless string of privileges my father and his guests enjoyed upon arrival in Sin City, and this weekend trip in the fall of 1984 was no different. The men who had showed up unannounced to my dad's foreign exchange on the border of Tijuana had made good on their promise. Jefe would be treated like a king whenever he was in their realm.

The driver took our bags and opened the limo door for us. It was just a short drive to the corner of Las Vegas Boulevard and Flamingo Road. There, we were not dropped off at the front lobby. Instead, the limo pulled up to the players' entrance, a more discreet point of admission for high rollers, celebrities, and other special guests. Once we were inside, we didn't use the normal elevator banks either. That's because we were headed up to one of the penthouse suites, which were accessible only via a private elevator.

The elevator operator kept his eyes upward and averted from the VIPs, which in our case included two eighth-grade boys. The elevator zipped us up to the top floor, where each suite was attended by a staff of four. The staff members assigned to our suite were ready, waiting to see what we needed immediately.

"A hot-fudge sundae, please," I said. "What do you want, Beamer?"

We could ask for anything, and it would be there in less than five minutes.

"Burger and fries. Oh, and a milkshake," said Beamer, who loved coming to Vegas with me. Why wouldn't he? It was the shit. Everything about Vegas was over-the-top, beginning with the Sultan's Suite, where we stayed.

The enormous living room was like *Aladdin* meets *Scarface*. It was opulent, gross, and kinda cool all at the same time. In the center of the room, decorated with draped textiles and twinkling chandeliers, was a self-playing grand piano. But the real jaw-dropper was the set of wrap-around windows that offered sweeping views of the entire Strip. Each of the four bedrooms in the suite looked out onto Vegas. Even the Jacuzzi, which had a glass bottom, floated over the Strip, for Christ's sake. The place was magical, beautiful, and like nothing else I'd ever seen.

The Dunes was continuing to struggle financially as Las Vegas went through the identity crisis that marked its shift from mafia playground to family-vacation destination. But to me, it still felt like the hottest place in town. Something about its unapologetic decadence resonated with the greed-is-good ethos of the '80s. The hotel and its iconic sign even appeared in such cultural touchstones of the decade as *Knight Rider* and *Cannonball Run II*.

The real draw of the Dunes for us, though, was the royal treatment we received—all of it on the house. No perk was off-limits. When Julio Iglesias came to play Vegas, Jefe was even comped tickets and backstage passes for his entire staff of women. By that point, Jefe had fifty-three female employees. They attended the concert in shifts so that the exchanges would remain staffed.

Although he loved to look at anyone in heels and a skirt, Jefe didn't hire beautiful women to work for him out of a desire to make them into his or anyone else's personal harem. His staffing decisions were instead fueled by his obsession with profits, which he was determined to increase in any way he could. He figured good-looking tellers would only drive more clients into the place.

When each of his female employees arrived at her hotel room on Friday before the concert, she found a fruit basket, a box of Godiva chocolates, and a bottle of champagne—all compliments of the Dunes—plus an envelope with one hundred dollars courtesy of my dad. That was just the start of the fun. Jefe had reserved four booths front and center where the women enjoyed a lavish dinner, all the drinks they could drink, and of course the main course: Julio Iglesias. The Spanish singer was, hands down, the number one Latin star in the world at the time. The ladies were like giddy schoolgirls. My dad was the man in their eyes, thanks to the Dunes.

Another person who wholeheartedly appreciated PL Exchange's relationship with the resort was Nando. His whoring in Vegas was so great, it became the stuff of legends. From the stories he told about having five or six girls in his room and "partying" until eight in the morning, it was clear that my uncle enjoyed the Dunes like nobody's business.

My mom's trips to Vegas, on the other hand, were more G-rated—but no less pleasurable for her than Nando's carousing was for him. Not a gambler by nature, she might play slots for a while before growing bored. She also enjoyed the lavish suites, decadent dinners, and big shows, as my father's employees did. But her true passion was shopping.

She simply loved to shop for, and dress in, fine clothes. Shopping was how she'd met my dad, and his own elevated sense of style had been part of what attracted her to him. Throughout all the ups and downs in their relationship, one interest they always shared was a love of shopping. The high-end boutiques in Las Vegas that catered to customers just like my mom—women with money, whose husbands were busy gambling or off doing God knows what else—were her special corner of the Vegas playground. There, she reveled in the fashions of Halston, Hermès, and Yves Saint Laurent.

Because I was a kid, I couldn't take advantage of a lot of Vegas's offerings. Still, the Dunes was my playground too. My favorite friend there—and really anywhere—was Will Beamer, who had been my best friend ever since we met in kindergarten at Francis W. Parker. Beamer also came down to the ranch a lot, and it was there that he had become a favorite of Abuelo's.

It was during one of my birthday parties at the ranch that Beamer cemented his relationship with my grandfather. My mom had organized a pie fight for the party that day. As pies were flying among the kids, Beamer glanced over at my grandfather, who in that moment looked every bit the lord of the manor in his riding boots and immaculate cashmere V-neck sweater and turtleneck. With a devilish look in his eyes, Beamer ran and threw the pie square at my grandfather's back. Abuelo thought it was hilarious and repeated the story until his dying day, always ending with, "William. Love that kid!"

After we finished our snacks in the Sultan Suite, we would head down to the arcade, where we got to play all the video games we wanted. That, for us, was a big deal. Adolescent boys at the time, we were obsessed with video games—and boobs. We checked out a ton of nudie magazines while in Vegas—again, with assistance from the Dunes staff. Before my dad would head out to the casino or to dine at the Sultan's Table, he'd first hand a C-note to whomever was monitoring us from hotel security and say, "Buy the boys anything they want. I don't care what it is. Just buy it."

In Vegas, a security guy from the hotel monitored me twenty-four-seven—this was thanks to my mom. Although I didn't know it at the time, my personal security detail had been a nonnegotiable condition of my being allowed to go to the Dunes with my father. There was no way my mother was going to leave me in the care of my dad without a scaffolding of safety built into the trip. Although she submitted to my father in myriad ways, when it came to me, she did not hesitate to assert her power.

Ama loved me to death. And I felt the same way about her. Almost every night of the week, we could be found on the couch at our home in Bonita, watching our favorite sitcoms together. Even though she'd been a diligent and passionate student during her youth, she let me blow off homework because she wanted me right by her side in front of the TV. We were each other's comfort. And we were best friends. I could talk to her about anything. Our car rides were filled with endless conversations in which no topic was off-limits.

Once I was old enough to be interested in girls, I asked my mom what makes a man a good lover. Her answer didn't get into the technicalities of sex, but she also didn't flinch from the topic.

"Just listen to her," she said. "Never treat a woman as if she is less than you."

I took her advice at face value at the time. But in hindsight, I imagine she was not just talking about sex. She probably also hoped that I would become a better man than my father, who often belittled my mother. Even her father hadn't treated her as an equal. Instead, she had been eclipsed in terms of status by her brother, despite the fact that she would have been better suited than he was to take over the family business. Ama was a woman ahead of her time. She knew what her place was with her family and husband. But she also knew where women were headed in society, and she wanted her son to adapt.

My mother was always honest with me about her feelings, and she fostered equality in our relationship through kindness. Whether she was listening or talking to me, she always made me feel like an equal. She took my concerns and questions as seriously as if she were talking to an adult, and she never waved off any of my ideas because of my age. Above all, Ama was a kind soul. She taught me to treat people with respect, and she taught me that humanity is fundamentally good.

She reserved her anger for anyone who might hurt me, and that included my father.

The only circumstance that my dad truly feared would cause my mother to leave him was if he went too far with his attacks on me. He could not allow that to happen. If she were to divorce him, all his money would dry up. He'd put all his assets and bank accounts in her name in order to protect them, in case he got arrested. So while he was usually a dick to her, Jefe also knew not to fuck around when it came to my safety. That's why when she gave him instructions regarding my care, he followed them to a T.

And Ama was *very* specific in her instructions concerning our trips to Vegas. "Tell the security detail to give the boys everything they want, but they aren't to do anything too wild," she ordered. "No drinking or smoking. But if they want to look at smut, get them all the magazines on the newsstand."

She was a realist when it came to sex. In fact, she was one of the most progressive moms I knew, particularly for a Mexican mother. But it was precisely because of what had happened to her as a young woman—getting pregnant out of wedlock—that she wanted me to know everything about sex. There was no sense in hiding the facts. She'd wanted to have sex as a teenager, and she knew I would too. So she told me about condoms and eventually went so far as to hand them out to my friends.

Her approach with me was always direct, and this was no different when it came to the rules for when I was in Vegas. She told me I was not to go beyond the hotel's walls without permission—and she expected me to listen.

"*Te quiero mucho*, Pichito," she said to me. "Listen to your father. Your dad is going to be working, so when you are on your own, you have to be responsible. Stay within the bounds of what we talked about."

Despite the openness of our relationship, however, she never let on that she was having me tailed the entire trip. I didn't learn about this until later in life when she told me, "You were never alone."

I learned that around the same time she confessed to me the real details behind the first time I drove myself to school. Sixteen at the time, I'd thought I was the man, riding solo in my new Mercedes-Benz AMG S-Class. I remained clueless about the fact that my mom in one car, and my security guard Alex in another, were following from three car lengths behind me.

Boundaries—both those overt and those hidden—were how my mother showed me love. And so it was that, within my mother's prescribed limits, Will and I ordered a ton of room service in Vegas, went to the arcades, and jerked off to a pile of nudie magazines.

"Whatever you want" became, more or less, my family's mantra as our fortunes rose quickly with Dad's business. Jefe had been making money ever since he opened the foreign exchange on the border of San Diego and Tijuana. But the bank loan from Ricci made it possible for him to grow his business as big as he wanted. Within eight months, his empire expanded to fourteen locations along the border from California to Texas. He put at least one or two foreign exchanges at every major crossing between the US and Mexico.

The injection of money into Jefe's business had another immediate impact, beyond expanding it. His access to a huge supply of dollars also meant that he could be more aggressive than his competition when it came to his exchange rate. At an exchange, the lower the rate, the better the deal for the customer and the less money the exchange makes. In my dad's case, however, whatever profit he lost by devaluing his currency by one or two points was more than made up through the sheer number of his exchanges and the volume of money being exchanged.

Soon everyone from San Diego to El Paso knew that La Greca had the best rates.

My father never took his eye off all the little guys who popped up with their own foreign exchanges. He made sure that none of them offered customers a better rate than he did. Dropping his rates just a half a point could drive one of these exchanges out of business, so it didn't take long at all for him to become the biggest player in San Ysidro. There was only one other major foreign exchange on the border of Tijuana, and it belonged to Rocky De La Fuente.

Though they competed toe-to-toe throughout the years, my father and Rocky both enjoyed the rivalry and later in life even became good friends. Plus, according to my dad, Rocky had only 5 percent of the market. My dad had the other 95 percent. This meant that Rocky wasn't *really* a competitor. If this hadn't been the case, Jefe probably wouldn't have been quite so friendly.

Rocky was a very smart and savvy businessman who had a talent for finding profit in unlikely ways. In later years, in fact, he won two land-use lawsuits against San Diego that brought him more than $60 million. But sometimes he took his "talents" a little too far. At one point the FDIC—the government agency that insures deposits in case of bank failures—even barred him from participating in any institutions they backed.

More than anything else, though, Rocky was a character. Like all the good Mexican elites of his time, he was born in San Diego. This made him an American citizen, and between 2016 and 2020, he ran for political office more than a dozen times in elections. He's run for US Senate, for mayor of New York—even for president of the United States, on a ticket with Kanye West as his VP.

Rocky never did things halfway. This included the Christmas party he held for the staff of his foreign exchange at Mr. A's Restaurant in downtown San Diego in the mid-1980s—by chance, the same night my father was hosting a Christmas party at the same restaurant for *his* staff.

In true form, the rivals—who had at that point been competing for business for more than a year—talked shit to each other all night long.

"Let's be friends," Jefe taunted Rocky. "Allow me to buy you some real champagne. Dom Pérignon Rosé."

Rosé was not mainstream at that point, let alone rosé champagne. But my dad—despite not being a drinker—knew about the latest trends among the rich, thanks to his frequent trips to Vegas, where wowing high rollers was a full-time profession. Jefe was well aware that Rocky would think he was making fun of him.

"Don't fuck with me, La Greca," Rocky barked.

"You're a heathen."

"You're full of shit."

"You really think I'm full of shit?" my father said. "Let's make a bet. If I order Dom Pérignon Rosé and there is no such thing, I pay for your staff's dinner. If the sommelier brings it out, you pay for mine."

Rocky knew my dad well enough to know he hated to lose money more than anything else. But at this point in the contest, which was taking place in front of his entire staff, it would have been worse to back down than to lose and foot the bill for PL Exchange's Christmas party.

"Can I order six bottles?" my father said.

"Order however much you want. It doesn't exist."

My dad ordered ten bottles of the champagne. He had every reason to be confident. After he first learned about the champagne in Vegas, he had asked the sommelier at Mr. A's if the restaurant carried it. The sommelier had answered that they didn't but said he'd be more than happy to oblige such a fine customer as Mr. La Greca, and then he'd promptly ordered a case. As was generally the case with whatever situation my father got into, he went into the bet with Rocky knowing that the deck was stacked in his favor.

When the waiters popped the corks on those bad boys, the women who worked for my father at the exchanges, now sitting at their tables, laughed before sipping the pink bubbly. Rocky was humiliated, but there were no hard feelings. Everyone was making plenty of money. Indeed, about four years later, when our families coincidentally ran into each other while in Florence, Italy, we decided to spend the rest of our vacations together.

My family had invited my friends Jimbo and Trevor along on that trip. While we were all in Sardinia, Rocky went out with my friends and me. One night, after spotting a group of beautiful women sitting at a bar, he said, "Boys, it's time to teach you how to pick up women using your words and looks." Then he said something I'll never forget: "Luckily, I don't have to worry about that anymore, because I have *check* appeal." After that trip, when the priest told me I needed a godfather for my confirmation, I decided to choose Rocky.

My father's appreciation of women was not as lascivious as Rocky's, but it was no less calculated. As the exchanges along the border had expanded, Jefe's staff had ballooned to as many as sixty employees, and nearly all of them were women. There were only two exceptions: Angelo and Alfredo.

Angelo had remained my dad's right-hand man ever since my mom planted him in Portofino. He was now Jefe's general manager, assistant, confidant, and all-around henchman. He was also a very big dude. My dad liked this because Angelo looked like he was a bodyguard who was driving my father around and doing his bidding. Which, in a sense, he was. His job description was basically to do whatever my father asked. "Angelo, go fucking find out," and "Angelo, go find this asshole," were constant refrains. Angelo figured out a way to find anything or anyone my dad needed, whenever that was needed, no questions asked.

The problem with Angelo was that he had a very serious alcohol problem. This was a problem not just for Angelo but also for my dad. Jefe couldn't stand drunks, but he loved Angelo. So like many people who find themselves in relationships with others who suffer from addiction, my dad found himself in a constant cycle of anger, reconciliation, and disappointment.

Catching Angelo drinking in the morning, my dad would shout, "Get the fuck out of here, you drunk! You're fired!" Two days later, he'd call back and say, "Angelo, I have something for you to do." And so Angelo was rehired. My father thought he could keep Angelo from drinking by tasking him out. In his own selfish way, my dad cared about him.

But a person can't cure alcoholism by staying busy. This is where Alfredo came in. Alfredo essentially became Angelo's secretary. One day, my dad noticed that Alfredo, an entry-level accountant who was working for my father's accounting firm, was the brains behind that business—and so he poached him.

Alfredo was a diamond in the rough whose value was evident to my father. Tall and skinny, Alfredo was the stereotypical nerdy accountant who wore the same khakis and shoes for six years because he believed in saving money—a detail not lost on my father.

"You look like shit," Angelo told Alfredo one day. "You better buy some clothes if you want to stick around." A couple of flashy suits and a few pairs of Italian shoes later, Alfredo had been made over in my father's image. Whereas Angelo was big and fearless, Alfredo was quiet and subservient. He was also very smart with money, which made him essential to the foreign exchange.

There was one other person who was essential to the business, and that was Lupita, the exchange's real general manager. Since his staff was made up entirely of women, Jefe wanted to have a woman manager so there would be no blurring of the lines between business and pleasure. He didn't trust that either Angelo or Alfredo could maintain professionalism. (He wasn't wrong in his suspicions. Despite his best efforts, both men cheated on their wives with the tellers. At least, though, the men weren't in control of the women's careers.)

Women made up the backbone of my father's business. He positioned those he trusted most along the Texas border locations in Laredo,

Ciudad Juárez, and Tecate. These employees were his eyes and ears, and they had his back forever.

A no-nonsense married mother of two whose bob hairstyle and business attire perfectly mirrored her practical style, Lupita enjoyed managing the female tellers. She loved that they all looked up to her. She was the only one who could keep my dad in check. She did this by walking the fine line of giving news to him straight, all while refraining from threatening his manliness. After closing the door to his office so she could talk to him in private, Lupita would begin every hard discussion with the same disclaimer: "Señor La Greca, don't fire me, but I have to tell you . . ."

As he'd done with Angelo and Alfredo, my father saw underappreciated potential in Lupita and gave her a chance she would not have gotten elsewhere. Though I wouldn't call Jefe a feminist, it is true that hiring a female general manager in Mexico was at the time a revolutionary move. He provided women with opportunities they could not find elsewhere in Mexico's chauvinist culture. He also manipulated them with his charisma. Whether out of appreciation or because he'd charmed them, their loyalty to their boss was unshakable.

"When it comes to money, always go for a woman," my dad told me. "They're the only ones you can trust."

Implicit faith in females was perhaps the one trait my grandfather and dad shared. A team of women handled all the finances at the customshouse brokerage too. Agreeing that women were the superior sex when it came to matters of money, however, was where the common ground between them began and ended.

By 1985, Abuelo and Jefe's mutual enmity hadn't abated, but it had changed. That's because the power dynamic between the two men was shifting. For the first time, my dad had the upper hand financially and, even worse, psychologically. My dad had gotten into my grandfather's head. Abuelo had a hard time accepting that my father's easy-buck ways seemed to be winning out. He even found himself questioning his cornerstone belief in the necessity of hard work. That's because my father's fortune was rising meteorically during the worst economic period in Mexico's history. His grip on the foreign-exchange market even earned him the moniker "The King of the Peso." Trying to prove his prominence, he spent lavishly, and our family's lifestyle went into overdrive.

First came the cars. Cars were my dad's jam. Even before he hit it big with the exchange, driving a nice car had been as crucial to my father's identity as wearing a tailored suit. When he got his first Lincoln—standard issue for the modern Italian con man—he was the happiest man on the planet. He loved leasing cars, and he loved breaking the leases. As expensive as the practice was, he did it all the time. Getting into a fresh new car was a matter of his ego, not of his pocketbook. When it came to cars, he was like a child: always wanting the newest, shiniest model. Although he traded cars many times throughout my early childhood, however, he stayed faithful to Lincolns, returning to them again and again.

One particular Lincoln, the Mark V Diamond Jubilee in baby blue, was his baby. That is, until the Dunes deal. That's when he upgraded to his first Mercedes, a champagne 380 SEL. That was a big day for him. What he *really* wanted was a Ferrari—his first car love—but he didn't get one. He said he didn't want to look stupid as an old man, driving a young man's car. I thought he was crazy and told him so: "Old men are the only ones who can afford Ferraris." But my dad didn't listen. Still, he was vain as hell, so he became a Mercedes guy forever.

The new car he bought my mom, though, was the real showstopper—a Rolls-Royce. There was really no other option. He wanted her to have a car that was meant to have a driver, but he wasn't about to buy her a limousine. That would be too cheesy. At the time, San Diego didn't have the clientele to support a Rolls-Royce dealership. The closest dealerships were in Los Angeles and Newport Beach. Like everything else, the title for the car would be put in my mother's name. This meant that she had to be present at the dealership when he purchased it. My parents' anniversary was coming up, so my dad told my mom they were going to celebrate it in Newport, a place they loved to spend the weekend, staying at the Newporter Inn and shopping at Fashion Island.

The big surprise was Ama's gift, which she learned of when we paid a visit to the Rolls dealership on Saturday afternoon. My mom flipped out and had no problem choosing the car she wanted: a white Silver Spur with a tan top and tan interior that included a fold-down table in the back seat. The car was jaw-droppingly gorgeous.

Now came the haggling. My father loved to negotiate. It was one of his life's great passions. Whether he was buying a straw hat from a peddler on the beach or a Silver Spur in Newport, he always bargained. Jefe worked over the appalled Rolls-Royce salesman until finally the poor man brought the price of the car down to $115,000. *Great!* I thought. *He got a deal. Hand over the money.* But no, Dad always had to push things right up or, more often than not, over the boundary line. "Fuck it," he said under his breath. "They have way too many cars here. I'm going to ask for more."

He returned to the beleaguered salesman and made a final offer of $105,000. But the dealership wouldn't budge on their original offer. Normally, he would have backed out and waited for them to call with their counteroffer. But he *had* to walk out of that dealership with a Rolls. It was my mother's anniversary gift.

Jefe had a cashier's check ready to go in his hand—one that he'd had made out beforehand with his lowball walk-away number. But instead of handing it over, he asked if the dealership would accept a credit card. Yes, they would, so he gave them his American Express Platinum card with no limit. Credit cards charge 2 to 4 percent to the vendor, though, whereas there are no fees with a check. The salesman quickly pivoted and offered to bring down the price if my dad paid with the check, but Jefe wasn't having it.

"Too late," he said. "I'm going to take the AmEx rewards instead."

My dad was that kind of motherfucker. The dealership got the message. He got a much different reception when he came back a month later to buy Nando a convertible Corniche and then again when he bought another Silver Spur for Abuela to match her daughter's. From the moment my mother and grandmother first exited the Rolls at Neiman Marcus, where they'd gone for a shopping trip, they were hooked on feeling like movie stars, which is exactly what riding in that Rolls did for them.

Jefe didn't limit his largesse to luxury automobiles. I got anything I wanted, too, and I didn't even have to ask. I was given an "allowance" to buy whatever caught my eye. But it wasn't really an allowance, because I was told to come back and get more money if I ran out. I also was given stuff I never would have asked for, like a gold Rolex, which—to state the obvious—is not a normal gift for an eighth grader.

Dad showered Ama and Abuela in flashy jewelry he picked up on his many visits to Vegas. One day, feeling flush, he thought nothing of dropping a quarter of a million dollars on a diamond necklace that my mom came to call her "ugly diamond." She wasn't, however, calling the single round sixty-five-carat diamond that hung from a gold chain "ugly."

"If I look like shit, I put that big motherfucker on," she explained about the massive rock nestled right above her ample chest. "Then people are either looking at my tits or looking at the diamond, but no one's looking at my face."

Ama and I also loved our beautiful house in Bonita, where we had a pool, great backyard, guesthouse. It was a lovelier home than most people could ever dream of owning, but Jefe wanted more. He wanted to buy a bigger house in a better neighborhood—yet still within striking distance of his offices, so he wouldn't have a commute to work. By the spring of '85, he'd already found the perfect place: Coronado.

The island across was only a two-mile drive from the high-rises of downtown San Diego, but with its beachy atmosphere, Coronado might as well have been worlds away. Originally developed as a beach resort town, the small enclave was ultra-affluent and exclusive. Dad found a house in a gated community with its own boat slip on the property so that we could park our boat right in our very own backyard. We didn't even have a boat.

Ama protested my father's plan immediately. "This is home," she said of the house in Bonita.

Home meant something entirely different to my mother than it did to my father. For my dad, home was the place he returned to after a long day at work and after hanging with his pals at Mr. A's. For Ama, home was a place where she could feed my friends and me. She loved to cook; her way of giving was through food. When the boys came over—including Trevor, Beamer, and Apple—her first question was always, "Want some pasta?" The answer was always a chorus of "Yes!" Ama's pasta was legendary. After baseball games, she fed the entire team. She had designed her dream kitchen in Bonita with four ovens, eight gas burners, and the best kitchen appliances known to man, so that she could prepare meals for teams of hungry boys and throw lavish parties for my dad.

Home was also a place where her son could play safely. The backyard had been built for me with that goal in mind. The large rolling lawn was surrounded by a concrete walkway so that I would have a place to ride my bike. I didn't need to ride in the streets because I had my own bike path, complete with a little lip for jumps. That yard was a magical place, and when I was there, I never got bored by my own company.

Ama also had a basketball court built behind the guesthouse, and I spent countless hours shooting hoops. She practically had to drag me in at night. Especially if my dad was home early from work, I escaped out there. When I was safely out on the basketball court, I couldn't make a mistake that would incur my dad's wrath.

So, no. Ama and I didn't want to move to or live in Coronado. But Dad was crafty in his approach.

"I understand," he said. "I'll buy the house in Coronado as a weekend place. We have the money. We'll go there, play in the water, and enjoy the boat. Picho, you'll have fun. I'll have fun."

How could my mom and I argue with that? My dad, however, believed that after only one visit, he'd have us right where he wanted us, and he was right. From the moment we ascended the soaring, iconic San Diego–Coronado Bridge—sailboats bobbing below it like toys in a tub—we could feel the relief of having left the bustle of the city behind us, willingly trading it for the tranquility of the ocean.

The salt air, swaying palm trees, sparkling beaches, and manicured greenery made for a beautiful community. And the place Jefe had found? It was insane. In addition to the 4,500-square-foot home that had been built on it, the property even had a running stream that ended in a little waterfall. My dad had played us perfectly. Our family went there for a weekend stay and never left again. The jewels, cars, clothes, parties, and trips my dad had long footed for us were all extravagant. But nothing spelled out our new wealth more clearly than our move to Coronado.

My dad had become what he always wanted to be—a high roller. As if to drive the point home, he bought a self-playing baby grand, like the piano in the Sultan's Suite that my friends and I thought was so cool. The white piano was lacquered to so high a finish, it practically glowed from its place in the main living room. It was a reminder that Jefe was wealthy, and Jefe showed off his wealth any chance he could.

My family happily accepted all these lavish gestures. Ama, Abuela, Tio Fer, and I enjoyed without reservation the money, gifts, and trips. There was only one of us who didn't partake in the regular celebrations of excess: Abuelo. He wanted nothing to do with the Dunes. Yes, my grandfather was jealous that his no-good son-in-law was now the center of familial beneficence, but he also hated Las Vegas.

Don Fernando was not a gambling man.

CHAPTER 7

DÓLARES CONTROLADOS

Beamer, Stat, Apple, and I were having a blast during a weeklong ski trip over our February break from school. My parents had rented a house right on Heavenly Mountain in Lake Tahoe for a special trip for my friends and me.

Apple, who went to Francis W. Parker with Beamer and me, would grow up to become an accomplished lawyer in San Diego, although you never would have guessed it back then. He was the craziest out of all my friends, to the point where our maid gave him the nickname El Diablo. He played a key role in us figuring out how to sneak into the small outdoor ice-skating rink near the Tahoe condo so we could play broomball all night after skiing all day. The experience left me feeling blissed out.

My dad, on the other hand, was having a terrible time. He couldn't ski, and because he had heart and high-blood-pressure issues, he didn't do well at the high altitude. With nothing to do, Jefe was going stir-crazy. Feeling bored out of his mind, he told my mom he was headed off to one of the clusters of casinos on the Nevada side of the lake. Ama didn't want him to go.

"This is a vacation for Picho, for the family," she said. But he wouldn't hear of it. When Jefe made up his mind, there was no stopping him. Still, on his way out, she begged, "Please don't play hard."

That was a naive request. My dad didn't know how to play any other way. His two games were roulette and baccarat. He tended to have fun at roulette, but he *won* at baccarat. At the Lake Tahoe casino, he sat down at the baccarat table where he played both hard and well.

Eventually the casino host approached my father to introduce himself and ask if there was anything Jefe needed. This was common practice at casinos, where hosts wanted to make players on a hot streak comfortable—so comfortable, in fact, that they would start to lose. Jefe introduced himself with a fake name and said he was fine but assured the host that he would let him know if anything came up.

Forty-five minutes later, the casino host returned and whispered in my dad's ear. "We know exactly who you are, Mr. La Greca. You have two suites upstairs waiting for you and an open line of credit at the table to do whatever you want."

The last thing anyone should want in a casino is an open line of credit. The risk of losing it all under those conditions—and I mean *everything*—is too great.

My dad called the condo after we'd come in off the slopes. "Oh, good, you're finally back," he said to my mother. "I'm going to drive and pick up you and the boys. I have two suites here, and dinner is comped. It's so much better here than up there."

Before my mom could protest, he was off the phone and on his way. He drove us down the mountain, and we arrived at the casino hotel, where my dad delivered on his promise to buy us an amazing dinner. My friends called it the "scampi dinner" because Apple ate four entrées of shrimp scampi. When it's on the house, why not?

After dinner, Mom and Dad went back to the tables while my friends and I went up to the room. There, we helped ourselves to the alcohol in the fully stocked bar in the suite. Four plates of buttery shrimp followed by a lot of liquor, however, is not a good combo. Apple wound up puking scampi out of the hotel window for forty minutes while the rest of us laughed our asses off at him. That is, we laughed until the room phone rang. I picked up. It was my mom.

"Get the boys and get down here now."

I didn't ask any questions. Her tone said it all. I hustled the drunk boys out of the room.

Ama was waiting in the lobby. She walked outside as soon as she saw us. We followed her.

"Your dad is a fucking asshole. We have to leave now," she said.

"Who is going to take us?" I asked just as the valet pulled up with our car.

"Get in the car."

It was dark, and it had started to snow. My mother didn't drive that much, even back in sunny Southern California. Now, she was white-knuckling a treacherous drive on a snowy road that wound up a mountain. It was a risk I knew she would normally never take with us. She was the den mom to my group of friends: constantly feeding us, keeping our secrets, protecting us. This behavior didn't make sense.

From the front passenger seat, I turned to look at my mother. With her hands gripping the wheel and her gaze glued to the road, she was crying without a sound. Her expression was so fixed, I wouldn't have known she was crying if it were not for the tears I saw rolling down her cheeks. I put my hand on her arm in love, compassion, and solidarity. She was trying to be strong, and I wanted her to know I was there for her.

I later learned what had happened back at the casino. My dad had been down a half million at the baccarat table when my mom stepped in.

"Get the fuck off the table," she said.

"Go fuck yourself," he yelled in front of everyone at the table. "I'm going to do whatever I want to do right now. So get away from the fucking table."

Jefe returned to the condo via a casino limo at eight in the morning. When he came in, he greeted my mother not with an apology but by throwing a briefcase on the bed. Inside, there was a little less than $1 million. The cash did little to lift Ama's crushed spirits. Her anger hadn't just been about my father risking so much money or even about how he'd humiliated her in front of strangers. This had never been meant to be a trip for my dad; it was supposed to be for my friends and me. On day two of the vacation, however, he'd made it about him. He couldn't stand for things to be any other way.

When my friends woke up, Jefe continued to show off his winnings. "A hundred for you. A hundred for you." He peeled off a C-note for each boy, going round and round until my buddies each had $500 in their hands to take home. They were super psyched, the uncomfortable events of the night before now completely forgotten. Mom and I were less impressed. My dad's apologies always took the form of a payoff.

While it was true that my father hated to lose money more than anything else on the planet, he was still a gambler at heart. The reward simply had to be big enough for him to be willing to take the risk.

So when he flew to San Francisco in late 1984 and arrived at Ricci's office, unannounced, Jefe had to believe he was paving the way for a huge payoff. He undoubtedly knew that he was taking the biggest gamble of his life. Showing up at the bank clearly violated the terms of Ricci's unspoken role as hidden conduit between PL Exchange and the Dunes. Even more daring was the request my father made that day: one he could only make face-to-face.

"Teach me how to launder currency."

As the King of the Peso, my father had created a large network made of Mexico's wealthiest and most powerful individuals. The country's disastrous economic slide had been ongoing for two years, and there was no end to it in sight. This meant that a steady stream of politicians, entertainers, journalists, and criminals flowed through Jefe's foreign exchange.

One relationship in particular had paved the way for my father to reach an even higher caliber of clients. He had exchanged a lot of money for Mexico's former president José López Portillo, and Portillo had then given a tacit green light to his friends to work with the Italian too. Jefe's circle included not just government types who were on the take but also millionaires and billionaires out of Mexico City, socialites, and celebrities.

As great as it was for my father's exchange to have these bigwigs as clients, their business also put him under a new kind of pressure: time. Now that he had a pipeline hooked up to a major US bank, product—dollars—was no longer his enemy. Speed was his enemy now. His difficulties stemmed from Mexican regulations that capped at $10,000 the amount of money an individual could exchange at any given time without getting taxed.

My dad's initial solution to this problem was to hire runners to cross over the border into Mexico and back again, each with $9,999 in pesos they had picked up from Mexican clients who wanted to change their money into dollars at PL Exchange. The couriers he entrusted to carry bags of cash into the US were teenage boys. All of them had American passports and were related to someone on Jefe's staff. Some were cashiers' nephews or brothers—the relationship didn't matter, as long as my dad knew the person. Angelo's kid was a courier. Even my uncle Nando would sometimes take a shift if needed.

"Fuck, I'll go and cross it," he'd say. Money was money.

Many of the wealthy Mexicans who were looking to change money had American passports of their own or could cross the border easily enough themselves, with their own money. But my dad's battalion of teens offered a service of convenience. Jefe was offering not just his guaranteed best exchange rate but service too. Despite my father's best efforts, however, $10,000 was a drop in the bucket compared to the millions of pesos his major clients wanted to exchange without any tax consequences. A $100,000 exchange took ten trips!

Jefe would offer a three-day, all-expenses-paid trip to the Dunes to important Mexican clients who were interested in changing large sums. Such a trip would keep a client entertained while he hustled to get upward of twenty couriers crossing each hour, each one carrying the maximum amount. And still, he could not keep up with demand.

"There has to be a faster way of doing it," my dad said.

Indeed, there was, and that way was to move the pesos across the border without alerting customs. Such an operation was out of my dad's depth. But he knew one man who did know how to make things like this happen: Ricci. After all, Ricci was the guy who'd pulled a bait and switch on Jefe with the bank loan that had really been an underground line to the Dunes. He and Ricci spoke the same underhanded language. At least that's what my father thought the day he barged into Ricci's office.

My dad was many things, but subtle wasn't one of them. He directly asked an already shocked Ricci, right there in Ricci's place of work, to teach him how to launder money. The move was beyond bold; it was insane. My father had seen the potential to make vast sums of money with this con. But he'd also wanted to take revenge on Ricci for his original sin. *Me vieron la cara de pendejo.* The banker had made a fool of him when he forced him into the Dunes deal, but now my father felt like he was in a position of power. Without my father's help, Ricci's whole scam involving the Dunes would fall apart. Jefe thought he held all the cards. He was wrong. Furious, Ricci kicked him out of his office and threatened to cut off his line of credit.

With his tail between his legs, my dad returned to his hotel. He had vastly miscalculated the odds. He'd thought he had Ricci by the balls. Now, he had put the future of his flourishing business at serious risk. He had no assurances that he could get a $30 million loan from another bank at all, much less at the same rate.

Three hours and two packs of cigarettes later, the phone in my dad's hotel room rang. It was Ricci.

"Come downstairs," said the banker, who was waiting in the hotel lobby. "Never, ever come to my office again," he snarled when my dad walked up to him minutes later.

My dad hung his head.

"Do you know anybody in customs?" Ricci then asked, having returned to the calm, even tone of a banker.

Jefe looked up. His whole face lit up, he told my mother and me later. Did he know someone in customs? Only Mexico's most powerful player—his father-in-law.

The scenario that Ricci had cooked up for my dad centered on a legal provision that allowed certain Mexican businesses to exchange pesos for dollars at a preferential rate. The businesses that could do this were the ones whose operations required them to buy goods in the US that weren't manufactured domestically in Mexico. This wasn't illegal. But if the goods that were being "purchased" at the advantageous rate didn't exist—except on paper, as a way to launder pesos at a better price—well, that was definitely against a law or two.

With this new system, clients would be able to exchange much more money at one time without incurring the heavy tax penalty that kicked in for any amount over $9,999. Plus, they would also get the preferential commercial rate, resulting in a financial benefit of which my father would certainly get a hefty cut. It was a win-win situation.

Critical elements, however, needed to fall into place if Ricci's plan to launder money out of Mexico was going to work. He needed a seal from customs to authenticate fake merchandise transactions and green cards—all of which Don Fernando could provide. The green cards would allow the clients to open bank accounts on the US side of the border, where their dollars would be safe from scrutiny from American regulatory agencies and future devaluation in Mexico.

It was imperative that my father convince my grandfather to partner with him; this relationship would be vital to his success. More to the point: without my grandfather's control of US/Mexican customs, the plan would not work.

That convincing, however, was easier said than done. The men's long-standing rivalry posed a major roadblock to their collaboration. An even bigger obstacle to getting Don Fernando to enter into a criminal scheme with his no-good son-in-law was the old man's insistence on running a respected enterprise. Jefe couldn't simply offer his father-in-law a chance to do business together. Don Fernando's pride would never allow him to enter a deal with the Italian, no matter how much he stood to benefit financially. No, my dad had to lure my grandfather into the scheme, and he knew how to do it.

His way in was through my uncle.

When Nando had gone to work for my dad at the exchange, this had done nothing but create a larger schism between my father and grandfather. He'd used my uncle as a pawn to get back at Don Fernando for refusing to include him in the customshouse brokerage business. Jefe had groomed Nando for foreign-exchange work, showing him the ropes of the business and paying him handsomely to do little more than sit in the office. During his time at the exchange, my uncle had even picked up my father's sense of style. At one time, he'd dressed more conservatively, like his father: Brooks Brothers suits and wing-tip shoes. Now, however, Nando wore snazzier Italian clothes. There was no doubt about it—my uncle looked up to my dad. And my grandfather hated that, which was exactly the effect my father had wanted.

Now, Jefe would use Nando as a pawn again. But this time, his goal was not to piss my grandfather off. It was to bring him into the fold. My father knew that this new operation provided the perfect opportunity for Don Fernando to keep a closer eye on his son's activities. But my uncle wasn't the only chip my dad had to play.

Though the collapse of the peso was the basis of my dad's growing fortune, it was absolutely killing my grandfather's business. As a Mexican customshouse broker, Abuelo made money off goods coming into the country. Now, because of the severe devaluation of the peso, the purchasing power of Mexican companies to buy goods from abroad had greatly decreased. At one time, Abuelo had crossed between four hundred and five hundred trucks per day. During the financial crisis, that number dropped to less than two hundred.

To add insult to injury, his son-in-law had taken every possible opportunity to flaunt his newfound wealth. At Christmas, my dad had given my grandma and mom some heavy-duty jewels and watches. Ama, Abuela, and Nando all received Piaget Polos. The heavy solid-gold watch favored by the jet set of the '80s was an expensive nod to the sport that my family had started to dabble in on the ranch. Although my dad had never been on a horse, he got a Polo watch for himself too. My grandfather didn't receive one, however, because, Jefe explained, Don Fernando didn't wear watches. This was true, but still.

And that wasn't the end of the pricey gifts. My dad also bought my mother and grandmother each a matching set of jewels. My mother's ring, earrings, and necklace were made of rubies, while Abuela's were set with emeralds. In my grandfather's eyes, it was one thing for my father to buy jewelry for his own wife. But when my dad gifted *his* wife the same, that really stuck in Abuelo's craw.

This was the backdrop to a family gathering that occurred sometime after his meeting with Ricci, which my dad chose as the moment when he would tap Don Fernando on the back.

"Fernandito is making good money with me," he said. "But we can make a shit ton more."

My grandfather was angry inside when my father said this, but on the outside, he appeared calm and quiet, as was his way. He didn't respond to my father right away, which was typical of his measured manner. However, Jefe had given him a lot to think about. Abuelo had a credo that he repeated to me many times when we were out at the ranch and when I visited him at work: "Pichito, always be on the right side of the law."

On the other hand, the customshouse business was sliding. His no-good son was making more money than he was, and his criminal son-in-law was showering his wife with jewels. This was the perfect storm that pushed my grandfather to renounce one of his major principles and accept a crooked offer from a man he loathed.

The whole deal was brokered over the next week through Germán, my grandfather's longtime faithful driver. Germán acted as an intermediary by carrying messages between the two men. This was necessary because although my grandfather was willing to consider the arrangement, he refused to say so to my father's face.

At the conclusion of the negotiations, the two patriarchs of my family—men who despised each other—finally went into business together for the first time. They still weren't friendly by any means. But now that they had a shared interest, they could at least be in the same room together without the interaction quickly devolving into an argument. Each of them held their disdain for the other inside.

My mom, on the other hand, could barely contain her happiness. She and Abuela were used to tiptoeing around their husbands' animosity for one another. They would always confer before events that required both men to be present. My mother would arrive to dinner with my dad on the later side of the evening, offering phony excuses, knowing that Abuelo would arrive and leave early so the men wouldn't have to spend more than a couple of hours in the same room.

Both my mother and grandmother were pleased with the new arrangement. Finally, here was the acceptance of her husband that my mom had been waiting for her father to give ever since the day she got married. As for Abuela, she had been jealously eyeing her daughter's increasingly opulent lifestyle. She had been more than happy to avail herself of trips to the Dunes with her daughter and lavish shopping trips and presents of jewelry, courtesy of her son-in-law. But it would be even better for her to be given those luxuries by her husband.

"We are going to come out stronger as a family," Ama told her mother confidently while the two women were getting their hair done at their weekly Thursday appointment. Wittingly or unwittingly, they were unaware of the illegality of the operation. Just as my mother had happily accepted my father's explanations during the early insurance scam years that he was involved in imports-exports, now she and my grandmother were content to believe that their husbands were "in business" together and leave it at that.

In some ways, my mom was right about our family. This was the happiest period in my extended family's life. My grandfather even went to Las Vegas a couple of times as part of family outings that included my uncle, grandmother, and parents—though he still hated the place. He never took up gambling but chose instead to explore the local area and learn about its history. He once took me to the Hoover Dam. By that time, I had been to Las Vegas dozens and dozens of times, yet I'd never visited the dam on the Colorado River, which had been built during the Great Depression.

"Let's go see how Las Vegas was actually created." Abuelo winked.

Money—when people have it—creates a lot of joy. Maybe that's why neither Ama nor Abuela asked too many questions about just how their husbands were making their money.

With Abuelo's help, Jefe set up a phony Mexican corporation to take advantage of the preferential rate offered to those who had to buy goods not made in the country. Whenever Jefe's fake company bought nonexistent equipment, the empty trucks entered Mexico through Don Fernando's state-sanctioned import-export firm. San Ysidro was Abuelo's closest border. He had customs officials along both sides of the border in his pocket. These officials had to log the record of the trucks crossing, but it was all a big show. If my grandfather didn't want a truck inspected, it wasn't inspected. "There's nothing to see in the trucks coming today," he would tell one of the inspectors in his pocket. "Your briefcase is going to get a little heavier."

Once the trucks crossed, the nonexistent US merchandise's supposed value was exchanged from pesos to dollars at the preferential rate. Then my father would sell the dollars at his foreign exchanges for the regular rate, pocketing the difference. Meanwhile, my grandfather expedited green cards for the clients so that they could open their own American bank accounts. The last step was to transfer the money that came from the "merchandise" from our account to theirs and then close our account. PL Exchange was a full-service operation. Later, Mexican newspapers would call the swindle *Dólares Controlados*.

Overnight, my dad's struggles to get money across the border disappeared. He no longer needed to find and coordinate teens to cross the border ten times a day carrying the backpacks filled with $9,999.

There were many laws broken in Dólares Controlados, but for Abuelo, abusing his Seal of Customs came with the greatest risk. The seal was the bureaucratic magic wand that made the whole con work. A tool of great power, the seal offered proof that real goods in real trucks were crossing the border of a real country. In fact, the trucks were real but the merchandise wasn't. Even in a nation as corrupt as Mexico, use of this seal was not a privilege to be trifled with. My grandfather knew that this transgression—faking trade between two countries—would be hard to bribe his way out of, if he were caught.

Up until then, the most illegal thing my grandfather had ever done was smuggle exotic animals for the private zoos of eccentric wealthy people. Such a transgression wasn't on any government's radar for prosecution. Yes, his role in Dólares Controlados was by far the most illegal thing he had ever done.

Abuelo rationalized his newfound criminality by telling himself that other people did much, much worse. There were coyotes who smuggled human beings across the border in appalling, sometimes life-threatening conditions. Drug mules carried over cocaine and marijuana to fuel the addictions of Americans. Unlike them, he wasn't hurting anyone. He was hardly doing anything at all. A few strokes of the pen here and there, a stamp mistakenly applied to some papers. As he sat at his desk overlooking the border, he was convinced his actions had no direct impact on the economy and so were of no consequence to anyone.

Champagne problems, Don Fernando thought as he waved through another empty truck.

CHAPTER 8

THE UNTHINKABLE

My dad walked out of the office and hopped into the car where German was waiting to drive him to the TJ airport to pick up a new client. When they arrived, they were quickly waved onto the tarmac. Germán, who picked up all of PL Exchange's big clients at the airport, was there so frequently, he might as well have been an employee. Jefe, however, went only on days when he met new clients. Today, they were going to pick up the number two in the Arellano cartel.

Although this new client was a top member of one of Mexico's most violent and dangerous criminal organizations, my father didn't veer from the routine followed with all their important customers. Germán took the man's bags—one filled with clothes, the other with money—and put them in the trunk. Then it was off to Abuelo's customshouse building on the border. During the ride, the men exchanged the typical Mexican pleasantries, throwing out names until eventually finding someone they knew in common.

Once they were inside the customshouse, my father guided the new client to the conference room, where they would collect all the information they needed to get him the necessary American government–issued document in order to open up a bank account in San Diego. Abuelo walked by but didn't greet my father or even make eye contact. He didn't pay much attention to what the men were doing, but he was well aware of what was going on.

Next, Germán took the man upstairs to the fourth floor, where a passport picture agency operated rent-free. The convenience was worth the cost. Just next door, also conveniently located, was the building that housed US visa, green card, and passport operations.

Once my dad had everything he needed from the new client, he said, "Germán will cross with you into San Diego so you can get settled in your hotel. Then perhaps a little breakfast? Germán will take you to a beautiful place overlooking the water. Then whatever you want. A trip to the zoo?"

While Germán shuttled the client around for the day, indulging his every whim, PL Exchange was grinding away. By the end of the day, the visa for the member of the Arellano cartel was ready and in the hands of Germán, who took the man to a friendly bank in San Diego to open an account. After the client had signed on the dotted line, the exchange transferred in his money.

The cartel member wasn't the only big client that day. As outlandish as it sounds, my dad could launder money for an Arellano brother at the top of the hour, for the head of the Mexican IRS at the bottom of it, and—in between the two—for the editor in chief of a major Mexican publication. This was business as usual for PL Exchange, which my dad turned into a seamless, one-stop shop for wealthy and powerful Mexicans who wanted to turn their currency into dollars. It didn't matter who a client was. Jefe did not discriminate when it came to money.

Jefe's clients could be sworn enemies, but they all had one thing in common: they wanted to launder their Mexican currency, which was continuing its stunning plummet. The peso's downward trajectory that started in 1980 with twenty-three pesos to the dollar had spiraled down to more than 350 pesos to the dollar in 1985. (The decline would continue until it hit a whopping 3,000 pesos to the dollar before the government issued new currency in 1993.)

Mexicans were steadily moving capital to the United States, where it could be protected from Mexico's hyperinflation, and with the power of my grandfather's connections and customs seal behind him, my dad was contributing to this mass exodus. The VIP customers at the exchange were all capable of getting their own visas or green cards, and they could have opened up their bank accounts in the US, but the process would have taken anywhere from five weeks to three months. My grandfather could get it done in three to four hours.

On those rare occasions when Abuelo wasn't able to get the necessary documents in time for the money transfer, my father would simply deposit the client's funds into an American account under his name, or my mother's name, or my uncle's, or even mine, since we were all US citizens. I had at least twenty bank accounts under my name, despite the fact that I was in middle school. The clean new American dollars would sit in our accounts until the client had the necessary documentation to open up their own. It was a matter of convenience more than anything else. The clients were going to get their money laundered. They were going to get American bank accounts. These little touches just expedited the process and made the whole thing feel seamless.

Sometimes instead of getting their money deposited into a bank account, the client preferred to make a property purchase. Real estate, which could be listed under a trust rather than a name, was a good way to minimize attention that might otherwise be caught by big sums of money coming into the US because, frankly, a Mexican client depositing millions in an American bank account doesn't look that great. Such activity could raise flags about the bank account owner's identity, where the money came from, or how it got there.

With his clients' approval, my dad purchased homes, cars, and boats with laundered money, signed over the deeds to shell corporations or family trusts, then jumped out of the transaction. A person had to be flexible in this business. Some clients wanted a mix: a couple of properties, a couple of bank accounts.

Although he was now working firmly on the wrong side of the law, my grandfather brought the same precise attention to money laundering that he had to every other aspect of his customshouse brokerage business. The whole operation ran like clockwork. But its success still hinged upon the bank deposit landing in San Ysidro every Thursday.

Even more important than the arrival of two Brinks trucks carrying millions from the B of A each week was the return of the money by PL Exchange before the end of the month. There were no penalties if Jefe returned the money to the bank in that amount of time, which he always did. That is, until about a year and a half into his sub-loan arrangement with the Dunes. Then came a day when the Vegas casino couldn't make its payment to my father's exchange in time.

The news threw a major wrench into my family's well-oiled machine. Suddenly Jefe was in financial trouble. *Big* financial trouble. The loan agreement stated that if he was a week late repaying the loan, he would have to pay interest and a late penalty fee. That could easily run upward of $7 million in cash, which my dad did not have.

"I've got to pay this loan very soon," Jefe told the Dunes' rep.

"That's your problem," the rep said.

There wasn't much more to the conversation. Maybe the Dunes had had a bad weekend on the floor, or perhaps they'd taken huge losses in a boxing match upset. My dad didn't ask why the Dunes couldn't pay the money back. He played it cool with the casino, because he knew these were dangerous guys. Plus, what would prying into their business do for him? They weren't paying up, no matter what he said.

Jefe couldn't turn to Ricci for help either. As the middleman for an illicit deal between the casino and the bank, Ricci couldn't acknowledge the relationship or treat my father with favoritism. But my dad needed to do something. The last thing he wanted to do was lose credibility with the bank. If he screwed up his line of credit with the bank, no other financial institution would touch him with a ten-foot pole. And he would still owe the money.

Once he got over the shock that the unthinkable had happened, my dad went into a panic. He didn't know what to do. He was frozen, and my father was not one to freeze. He was mad as hell, but there was no one for him to yell at. He didn't even involve Abuelo or Nando. He kept anything to do with the Dunes very close to his vest. He was backed into a corner. The truth would come out only much later, after Jefe's fix had landed our whole family in hot water.

For twenty-four hours, he worked through every possible move on his own. He needed to make the money back, and quickly. Stressed and lost in his thoughts, at times he had one cigarette burning in each of the two ashtrays he kept on either side of his desk and a third in his hand as he paced the length of his office.

Again and again, he went over the facts. But no matter how he approached the problem, he always came to the same conclusion. If he was going to save his own neck, he was going to have to cross someone. The question was, who could he afford to piss off? Whose anger would cause him the least repercussions?

Jefe feared criminals, like the goons who secretly pulled the strings in Vegas. But he didn't fear politicians. He especially didn't fear Mexican politicians, because he knew firsthand that they could all be bought. And my father had a close relationship with one of the most corrupt officials in the history of a government riddled with shady dealings: José López Portillo.

Back when he assumed the presidency in 1976, people had held high hopes for the tall, strapping, and charming leader, who at the time signaled to both the business world and the public sector that he was going to take the right steps to dampen inflation. Fast-forward to his exit from office in 1982, when Mexico was on the precipice of economic ruin. Despite the discovery of vast petroleum deposits in the Gulf of Mexico four years earlier, the government had become so bankrupt—thanks to López Portillo's inept leadership—that it couldn't even pay the interest on its foreign debt, which had ballooned to more than $60 billion.

As if driving his country into the ground with bad economic policies wasn't bad enough, the president had had the gall to brazenly enrich himself and his family members in full view of Mexicans who were suffering from a devalued currency and hyperinflation. The media widely reported on his outrageous real estate acquisitions, including a $2 million villa in Acapulco that he bought for one of his mistresses and a five-mansion family estate in one of Mexico City's wealthiest suburbs. Situated atop a hill overlooking the city, the property became known as "Dog Hill," a sarcastic reference to the president's empty promise earlier in his administration that he would "fight like a dog" to maintain the peso's value. López Portillo was so reviled by the Mexican public after he stepped down in 1982 that he lived mostly in Europe for a time, later slinking back into the country so as to avoid the very vocal accusations hurled against him.

None of that bothered my dad in the least. López Portillo was okay by him. More than okay. He was a prized client. The public perception of the president was on the mark: he had a ton of money to launder. Jefe exchanged the pesos not only of López Portillo but also those of the former president's wife *and* mistress. López Portillo's wife, Carmen Romano, did business with PL Exchange, as did his mistress, the actress Sasha Montenegro. All three members of this lucrative love triangle had multiple accounts with my father's exchange, and the parties were kept separate from one another during their interactions using various levels of secrecy.

So my father pulled out all the stops whenever he had a chance to show the president a good time. That, of course, included trips to the Dunes, for which my dad personally oversaw every detail. He traveled to Las Vegas to make sure that the check-in went smoothly; that the suite was immaculate and filled with all the amenities; and that the restaurant reservations were accurate, the beauty-parlor appointments booked, and the hookers lined up. Only when he was satisfied that these and other details were set up properly would he fly home.

This kind of attention wasn't just reserved for López Portillo. Relationships mattered a great deal to Jefe. He could read people through their smallest tells, like a twitch of the lip that meant someone was mad or a note in the voice signifying that my father had won a negotiation. As insensitive as the Barker in Brioni could be, he was able to read others very easily. While cultivating these relationships with powerful people, he took meticulous care in ensuring that they all were treated like kings when he invited them to the Dunes. *Powerful* didn't necessarily mean that a client was high up in the government or even that they had a lot of money. Dad sent a lot of reporters (he changed their money too) to the hotel casino as well. Whenever he did, he (or one of his trusted employees like Angelo or Alfredo) flew out to make sure the Sultan Suite was stocked with the right vices, just as he did with the former president of Mexico. My dad was prescient in his understanding that power comes in all forms. When you controlled the media, he liked to say, you controlled everything.

Once, back when his agreement with the Dunes was relatively new, my father arranged for López Portillo and his mistress to spend a weekend at the casino while they waited for their pesos to cross TJ and become dollars safely nestled in American bank accounts. While the couple was at the Dunes, Jefe received a distressing call from Carmen, the president's wife. The plan had been for her to stay back at home in Mexico City, but she had decided to change her plans and surprise her husband in Las Vegas. She wanted my father to make the arrangements, as he usually did for her and her husband. And she had no doubt Jefe would do *exactly* as she asked.

Like her husband, Carmen was used to getting what she wanted. She kept more than a dozen pianos in her home, which was a little excessive, even for an accomplished pianist like herself. But restraint was not her style. She wore colorful, formfitting dresses; large pieces of jewelry; high heels; and dramatic makeup to highlight her big green eyes and jet-black hair. On one trip to New York, she sent the salespeople in Bloomingdale's into a tizzy when she purchased $1,600 in beauty products, including the tester display. Carmen had the interior of the car she was driven around in specially fitted out with compartments to hold her makeup boxes and other things.

Jefe needed to comply with the lady's wishes and pronto. But the Sultan's Suite was currently occupied by her husband and his mistress. This was the kind of situation where my dad excelled. He quickly got López Portillo on the phone to tell him he had to lose the mistress because his wife was on the way. My father promised to fly Sasha to San Diego, where she would have a "very good time in my care" before sending her home.

Sasha—the B-movie star of such Mexican film classics as *Sex Makes Me Laugh* and *Snow White and Her Seven Lovers*—was my dad's kind of woman. She was a bombshell who didn't turn the volume down, ever. And neither did my father. They had had a great relationship, and he talked about her all the time. She would eventually become López Portillo's second wife, but even while she was still his mistress, my mother warned my father to keep his crush on the actress a little less visible.

"Pietro, watch your place," Ama said.

Right now, his place was to rescue Sasha and the president, whom my dad told, "We're switching you to another suite so there will be no evidence."

My father pulled off the whole operation so seamlessly—entertaining and spoiling both women into oblivion—that López Portillo never forgot it. The president gained a newfound confidence in the Italian, and the two men got really tight after that.

Although López Portillo's successor, Miguel de la Madrid, vowed to lead a moral revolution, Mexico's next president was also a client of my dad's. He had, after all, received *el dedazo*, the finger tap that signified he was the anointed successor of the PRI Party. The ruling political party, founded in 1929, had a monopoly on virtually every level of Mexico's government. (It wasn't until 2000 that the first PRI candidate lost the presidency.)

Still, the men were different. Whereas López Portillo was heavy on the charm and light on governing, de la Madrid was grim and kept himself busy implementing policies to turn Mexico into a first-world economy. Once in office, the former banking official and planning minister had responded to the mess of a country he'd inherited by raising taxes, slashing public spending, increasing interest rates, ending government subsidies, and selling off state-owned Mexican companies.

Both men skimmed off the top, but they did so in different ways. During the López Portillo administration, corruption had been gross; with de la Madrid, it became more elegant. De la Madrid was the first Mexican president to have studied in the US—he'd earned his master's degree from Harvard. He had, no doubt, observed how special interests maneuvered in Washington during the time he spent in America. Perhaps this was what inspired him to turn away from the freewheeling grab bag of his predecessor and instead cloak his graft—political kickbacks—in the form of government contracts and private-sector favoritism.

Not surprisingly, de la Madrid did not like my dad. The Italian's boisterous personality was not to the technocrat's taste. That didn't stop him from laundering money with him.

It was his relationships with not just one but two Mexican presidents that convinced my dad he could get away with the scheme he concocted to save the exchange after the Dunes didn't come through with its weekly payment. It was a crazy idea, even an insane one. But he couldn't think of any other way.

Pietro La Greca was going to devalue the peso.

The way the exchange system was set up, independent operations like PL Exchange might fiddle around with rates by less than a point in order to drive business. In Mexico, the exchange rate was dictated by Banco de México. But my dad's business was on the US side of the border. Because of that, he could, technically, exchange pesos for whatever rate he wanted.

My dad went to his back office, where a door led to the outdoor electronic board that advertised the exchange's rates to the cars that drove in and out of San Ysidro day and night. Then he walked to the sign and changed it. When he did so, he did the unthinkable: he dropped the rate of dollars to pesos dramatically. Mexicans, who were eager to get as many pesos per dollar as possible, wanted a higher rate. That meant he was going to lose a lot of business right away.

The news spread like wildfire along the border. All the other exchanges wanted to know what the Italian was up to.

"La Greca went down!"

"Something happened."

"It doesn't make sense."

Everyone looked at the newspaper to double-check the rate set by the central bank. They thought my father had made a mistake or lost his mind. They were used to La Greca giving his clients *better* rates, not worse ones, for pesos. At this time, Dad still handled the lion's share of the foreign-exchange business, with Rocky De La Fuente right behind him, followed by forty or fifty other small exchanges that divided the rest. Nervously, the owners of these tiny exchanges went back to work. They couldn't devalue their rates, too, because they didn't have the cash resources to support the loss in revenue on each transaction. But there had been no mistake. This had been step one of two in my father's risky play.

Those small exchanges, which kept their rates more favorable to those changing pesos, had so many clients that morning that it didn't take more than a few hours for them to run out of dollars. They didn't have the kind of money Jefe got from the bank, or anything close, backing them up. As the rest of the exchanges shuttered their doors, the first domino had fallen, just as my dad had planned, setting off the rest.

Next, he made a few phone calls to the reporters and editors he had in his pocket to give them a tip about what was happening down at the border. The result of his well-placed calls was a slew of articles the next day about "uncertainty in the market," which set off a panic. Another domino down. There was a rush at PL Exchange that day as Mexicans, having seen the news, worried that their unstable currency was about to go even lower. The fear of another devaluation generated an explosive amount of demand in a short amount of time. That was exactly my father's plan: create a rush on the exchange market to make back the money the Dunes owed before the bank loan was due.

My dad was basking in the pleasure of a scheme going exactly as planned and smugly smoking a cigarette at his desk when his secretary popped her head in the door.

"The president of Mexico is on the line," she said nervously.

De la Madrid's fury was unfortunate but also a predicted part of my father's plan. Jefe took a deep drag off his cigarette and then said, "Tell him I'm not here."

CHAPTER 9

TELLING OFF THE PRESIDENT OF MEXICO

My dad ignored the president of Mexico, who continued to call the office, for nearly a week. It took Jefe that long to make the money he needed to repay the Dunes loan back to the bank. Before that point, he didn't want to know what the consequences of his unilateral action would be.

De la Madrid had been tasked by his constituents with saving Mexico's economy from its unending nosedive. It was a difficult enough undertaking even before El Italiano woke up one day and decided to set the exchange rate himself. Once my dad had performed his little devaluation stunt, though, the president and the central bank of Mexico both knew just how powerful he was. It must have been terrifying to the Mexican government that the current exchange rate was based not on market conditions but on the whims of a crazy Italian on the border.

"What the fuck do you think you are doing!" the president yelled at my father when he finally picked up the phone.

The typically reserved de la Madrid went off on my dad. It was completely understandable to any rational human that he would be furious. But my dad was not rational. My father's temper was like a keg of gunpowder, and any attack on him—whether he deserved it or not, and even if the source of the attack was way more powerful than he was—was the only spark he needed for his rage to ignite.

Jefe's plan when he eventually spoke to de la Madrid had been to backtrack: to say that he had made a mistake, apologize, and return to business as usual—allowing the president to save face and stabilize the peso. But no one could go after my dad, not even the president of Mexico.

"I have you by the balls!" my dad barked at the president. "Go fuck yourself!"

Whatever volatility the president brought to that conversation, my father met it tenfold. He didn't care if fucking over de la Madrid ultimately meant he was fucking over himself. That's the kind of temper he had. My father never reversed course in life, but in this case, exploding was a particularly bad move. That was the very moment the president of Mexico began to quietly formulate a plan to take down my dad. His first move was to dispatch Carlos Hank to calm my father down.

Carlos Hank González, otherwise known as *El Profesor*, was an old-school Mexican politician-businessman. Famous for saying, "A politician who is poor is a poor politician," he had become one of the richest men in the country while serving in various positions, including as mayor of Mexico City, secretary of agriculture, and governor of his home state. He wasn't de la Madrid's man or even López Portillo's, for that matter. He was the man of whoever was in power.

Part of his own power lay in the fact that he held sway over many administrations. But not even Carlos Hank, whom de la Madrid had sent as his envoy, could get my dad to cool off and stop monkeying around with the rates and causing a panic in the press. When Hank met with my father—who continued to play with the rates after he repaid the bank loan because he liked the power and money—Jefe told him, "I will do whatever I want."

In the end, it took someone truly terrifying to mediate a truce between de la Madrid and my father—and that scary motherfucker was Mateo Garza.

Jefe had first met Garza through López Portillo years earlier. Before the former president began changing pesos for dollars with my father, he had needed someone to check out both the exchange and my dad. He sent Garza, a corrupt government official who kept his high-ranking position when de la Madrid took office. Perhaps this was because the new president thought he was doing a good job. Or maybe Garza simply knew too many powerful people to be removed.

His demeanor alone was enough to intimidate. A quiet man with thinning slicked-back hair, he commanded a room without saying much at all. The power he wielded and the myriad ways he could abuse that power didn't hurt either. At the airport, when he flew in from Mexico City, military guards and personal guards surrounded him as soon as he got off the plane, and everyone stood at attention: a clear testament to his authority.

My dad didn't kiss many asses, but he kissed Garza's ass. When the man came to town, he ran the show. "These are the things I want to do," he would tell my dad, and—no questions asked—my dad would set everything up. It wasn't just my dad who hopped to it for Garza. People bowed down to him wherever he went.

Garza owned a lot of property in Tijuana, which in the '80s was a hot tourism destination for Americans. Californians, including Hollywood's elite, poured into TJ, which was known for its jai alai, horse racing, beautiful restaurants (including one that was supposed to have invented the Caesar salad in 1924), and one of the most infamous red-light districts in the world. TJ provided opulence on the cheap—at least to foreigners, whose money went far in Mexico.

Garza owned multiple shopping centers and multiple office buildings in TJ, all of which he liked to check in on. As a child, I sometimes tagged along with my dad when he and Garza went on their walkabouts. The man commanded more respect than anyone I had ever seen. Everyone from receptionists to building managers freaked out upon his arrival. "Mr. Garza!" they cried. This was quickly followed by a show of obsequiousness.

Now, however, he trained his quiet force fully on my father.

"If you want to continue making money, Pietro, you can't do this," he said. He didn't have to say much more than that; such was the power Garza had over my dad. A lot of the exchange's earnings came through Garza and his contacts. He would bring in VIPs from Mexico City, whispering that if they wanted to change their pesos, "Go with Pietro." My father did not respect de la Madrid, but he did respect Garza. However, it was a respect that was based in fear. He knew that Garza could call on nefarious people. As I said, my dad didn't fear politicians. But he did fear criminals.

Jefe should have been more afraid at that point, or at least more careful. As it turned out, the truce Garza negotiated was one-sided. While PL Exchange returned to business as usual, de la Madrid quietly began an investigation into my father and his network. On the surface, it seemed like everything was rosy with the president. But behind the scenes, he pursued a vendetta. Slowly, methodically, and quietly, de la Madrid gathered evidence until the government was ready to make its case. It was not lost on my father, as he told me much later, that the warrant for his and Abuelo's arrest in May of '85 came one month after the last dollar from de la Madrid's own money-laundering efforts was transferred by the exchange into de la Madrid's bank account.

My first inkling that something was wrong came one day while I was playing *Donkey Kong Jr.* at the mall. I was so engrossed in my efforts to evade the fatal eggs of the game's Nitpickers that it wasn't until my security guard, Alex, tapped me on the back that I realized he was even there.

"Picho," he said, "it's time to go."

That was unusual. Normally it would be my grandmother or mom who fetched me from the arcade during our weekly Thursday afternoon outing to Fashion Valley Mall, San Diego's *it* mall in the '80s. During these trips, Abuela and Ama would go to the salon in the mall to get dolled up for their Friday night dates with their husbands. While they were getting their hair and nails done, I hit the mall's arcade. Other than *Black Knight*, a pinball machine I loved, I stuck to the standard video games hot at that time. I was a big *Donkey Kong, Donkey Kong Jr.*, and *Ms. Pac-Man* guy. Once they were done with the salon, my grandmother and mom would find me in the arcade, and then we would be off to get a banana split at Farrell's: an old-fashioned diner, ice-cream parlor, and candy store.

I didn't have a good feeling as I followed Alex out of the arcade. But when he kept walking out of the mall and toward the parking garage, I started to get really nervous. Then I spotted my mother and grandmother, also walking toward our car. My grandmother still had rollers in her hair. Even more alarming, however, was my mother's expression. She always smiled when she saw me. Now, her lips were pressed together tightly.

"Is everything okay?" I asked her, even though I knew it wasn't.

"Yes, honey. Don't worry."

I knew that my mom wasn't being honest. She also had to know that I could see she was lying. But I didn't need to pester her about why she was holding back on me. I trusted her enough to understand there was a good reason not to say more in that moment. My grandmother, mother, and I all remained silent for the entire forty-minute car ride home from the mall. Though I didn't know what was going on, I had a bad feeling in my gut.

When we rolled up to the house, we saw seven cars parked outside. In the area of Coronado where we lived, cars were rarely, if ever, parked on the street because every home had a multicar garage. Mom exhaled audibly. Now I was actually scared, though I was still unsure exactly why.

We went through the garage and in the back door that led to the kitchen, where my father, Nando, Germán, Angelo, Alfredo, and Lupita were huddled. When my grandma walked in through the door, someone said, "She's here." Suddenly the room went so quiet, I was sure everyone could hear my heart pounding.

Jefe locked eyes with Abuela.

"Señora Irma, I have bad news," Dad said. "Don Fernando has been arrested in Tijuana."

My grandmother froze. The former beauty queen in rollers, wife of one of TJ's most prominent and well-respected businessmen, didn't know how to react to news of her husband's arrest. As the implications sank in, she screamed at the top of her lungs, "No! No!"

Abuelo arrested? It came like a big punch to the gut. Like my grandmother, I was shocked and worried. I was also sad. I immediately started to miss my grandfather, my rock. I wanted to see him and to feel him reach out his hand and touch my head, like always.

As if suddenly possessed by an urgent errand, Abuela made a beeline for the door.

"Stop her," Jefe said to no one in particular. A member of the security detail blocked the door. My grandmother fell to her knees and wept.

My father turned to the rest of us and said, "We've got to get out of here right away."

Earlier that day, a mole in the Mexican justice department had tipped off my father, telling him that arrest warrants for customs fraud were coming for him and his father-in-law.

"Get the fuck away from the border," his source warned.

My dad didn't need to be told twice. He called my uncle, Angelo, Alfredo, and Lupita to tell them they better immediately cross the border into the US, where they would be out of reach of the Mexican authorities. Most important to reach was Abuelo, whose customs seal was the linchpin of the whole money-laundering operation.

"You need to get out of Mexico. *Now.*" My father didn't know exactly what was going on, but he knew that whatever it was, it would be much harder to fight on the wrong side of the border.

Sitting at his desk in his corner office on the first floor of the customs building, where his window was literally six feet away from US land, my grandfather listened to everything my father said, but he did not get up out of his chair.

"*Gracias, Pietro,*" he said. "*Déjame averiguar.*" Let me find out.

Abuelo was a man of few words, and he knew that his son-in-law was an exaggerator. But he also knew that my father was no fool.

As soon as he hung up with my dad, my grandfather called his good buddy, who was a high-court judge in Mexico. "Hey, do I have any problems that I need to worry about here?" he asked. The friend assured my grandfather that he was fine and that El Italiano was being typically dramatic. (This same "friend" had issued the warrant for Abuelo's arrest only hours before their chat. He had directly lied to my grandfather.)

"Get your stuff," my father barked at us now, "and get into the fucking car."

This was the first time I heard this order, but it wouldn't be the last.

My mother was a little gentler, guiding me to my room and saying, "Son, pack your clothes. Pack what you like. Pack what you need. If you forget something, don't worry about it. We can buy it later."

While I shoved some of my things into a duffel bag, I overheard Jefe talking to the other men in the kitchen.

"Everyone in this room, go to your family, grab them, and get back across the border to the US. *Immediately,*" he said.

Because his employees were lesser targets than he and Don Fernando were, my father believed they had enough time to leave Coronado, cross into Tijuana, gather their immediate family members, and return before they would be in danger.

When I returned to the kitchen with my stuff, I watched my dad hand thick envelopes to each of the guys. "After you're back, stay on the American side until you hear from me that it's safe," he said. "If you guys need more money, I'll send it." (All but two of his men listened to my dad and stayed out of Mexico. The two who didn't—they're both dead.)

We piled into three cars. The first carried my uncle, Jefe, and a security guard. Ama, Abuela, another security guard, and I rode in the second. Germán drove the last car, which was full of cash. We were all headed to the same place: the Beverly Wilshire.

A historic luxury hotel in the heart of Beverly Hills might not seem like a great place to lay low, but the Beverly Wilshire was a very comfortable place for our family. We knew the whole staff at the Wilshire, and everyone knew us. We had stayed there many times, and whenever we did, my dad dropped big tips left and right.

The first time we went to the hotel, a year earlier, we'd actually intended to go on vacation somewhere else. My father had booked the presidential suite at the Ritz-Carlton, Laguna Niguel. The suite, which had balconies that overlooked the Pacific Ocean in the bedrooms and living room, was spectacular. But for some reason, once we got there, my dad hated it.

Just as he'd done in so many other hotels, restaurants, department stores, and other places where he felt the service wasn't up to his standards, Jefe raised hell. There was no arguing with him, so we got back in the car and headed up to Los Angeles and the glamorous Beverly Wilshire, where my father got probably one of the nicest suites I had ever been in. The room was great, but I suspected it was really the hotel's location on the corner of Rodeo Drive that had prompted my dad's last-minute switch. My dad—who regularly spent a boatload on his Brioni suits—had made up the excuse that the room at the Ritz was crap so that, instead of being bored by the pool, he could go shopping with my mom.

Since that first stay, we'd returned to the Beverly Wilshire many times, usually while going on shopping vacations. Never before had we gone there to run from the law. Despite our circumstances, the hotel felt both luxurious and familiar to me as my dad, mom, uncle, grandmother, and I settled into a three-bedroom suite. At night, Germán slept in a second room next door to the suite. By day, they used the room as a war room to plot our next move. Two of our security guards had also come with us. One stood outside the door of our suite, and another was stationed downstairs in the lobby.

Apparently, though, no amount of security could keep us safe in such a high-profile place. On our second day at the Beverly Wilshire, I was at the hotel pool, where I had spent the entire day, splashing in the water, ordering ice cream, and relaxing in one of the surrounding cabanas. My dad was holed up in his room upstairs when he received an alarming call from an FBI agent. "We know that, right now, your son is in the pool at the Beverly Wilshire," the agent said. "If we know it, so does the Mexican government."

The call wasn't a threat but a tip-off. My dad, who feared the American criminal justice system more than anything, had made a habit of ingratiating himself to its many branches of law enforcement every chance he got. Sometimes that meant hiring ex-military and ex–FBI agents as well-paid security. Sometimes that involved providing crucial information for a sting. In every case, Jefe made sure the people involved knew whose side he was on: the US's. That's why, when the FBI heard chatter that the Mexican government was going to try to kidnap one of his family members as leverage for his surrender, they let my father know.

"You know what you have to do," the agent said before hanging up.

My dad did. He immediately purchased first-class tickets for the whole family. Within a few hours, we were headed to LAX.

The La Grecas were leaving the West Coast.

CHAPTER 10

ON THE RUN LA GRECA–STYLE

When we drove up to The Breakers in Palm Beach, I realized that up to that point, I had only *thought* I lived in the greatest state. The long landscaped drive, seemingly too perfect to be real, ended in what looked like another mirage: an imposing building, rising up from the Atlantic Ocean. The magnificent hotel looked like what would result if a Roman Renaissance villa met the Jazz Age. The porte cochere where we got out of the taxi was lined with Lamborghinis, DeLoreans, and Ferraris waiting for their owners to exit the vaulted lobby. Before making my first trip to the East Coast, I had naturally thought that everyone wanted to live in California. I now saw that I had been wrong.

My father, mother, abuela, and uncle had chosen the five-hundred-room legendary resort on 105 acres as our destination after the FBI tipped off my dad. It wasn't just that the Mexican government was after us. Jefe also worried about one of my family members potentially doing something dumb, like my grandmother crossing the border to see her husband or Nando—who could never say no to a party—heading into Rosarito. Jefe knew that if one of us was grabbed in Mexico, it was all over. The Mexican government was not above threatening our lives as leverage for a full confession from Abuelo: a confession that would send both him and my dad to jail for a long, long time. The farther we all could get from the San Diego–Tijuana border, the better for everyone in our family, except for my grandfather, who was already behind bars. Without leaving the country, Florida was as far from California as we could go.

We became the tightest-knit family of five that you ever saw. As we migrated east, everyone quickly got in line, like ducks in formation. Except instead of the momma duck leading the group, my father led the pack. Although he had the rest of us within earshot or line of sight almost all the time, we still divided along our usual mini camps.

The first camp was made up of my dad, who spent most of his time sequestered alone and on the phone. All day long he talked to Germán, who'd stayed back in California to keep the information flowing between Jefe and the team who continued to run the foreign exchange: Alfredo, Angelo, and Lupita. My dad was still running a business, all while trying to keep us safe and working to get my grandfather out of jail. His days were full, and he was stressed. Like the stereotypical CEO on a family vacation who can't step away from work, only more so: he was not, under any condition, to be interrupted.

Camp number two consisted of my grandmother and my mom. They spent all their time together, much of it hypothesizing on what exactly had happened. They didn't dare ask my dad anything. They knew they had to stay away from him and let him do his thing. Abuela had never been savvy enough anyway to inquire about the mechanics of her husband's and son-in-law's work. All she knew was that Don Fernando got trucks across the border—and frankly, she didn't care to know more than that.

My mom was not as naive as her mother. Though I'm not sure whether she actually wanted to know the truth of what had gone down, I do know that she understood better than anyone else how much my dad hated to be probed, even on a good day. Ask him more than one or two questions and he'd flip his lid.

And so the women were left to come up with their own answers, like conspiracy theorists speculating on secret plots. Before Abuelo's arrest, my father and grandfather had led my mother and Abuela to believe that they'd found a loophole that allowed them to exchange money using the commercial rate to their advantage. Having left out the part of the story where they falsely used a government seal to outright break the law, my father and grandfather convinced the women they were just being smart businessmen.

It was harder to keep up the collective lie when, almost a week after Abuelo's arrest, the *L.A. Times* reported on the arrest of seven men—including Tijuana bank branch managers, a Mexican customs official, and, of course, my grandfather—in an "intricate $34 million currency fraud scheme."

The seven men allegedly participated in a scheme to obtain the American currency at the preferential rate for about 215 pesos per dollar, then sold those dollars at a San Ysidro currency exchange for about 245 pesos per dollar, the current market rate, the article stated. It went on: Mexican authorities believe the seven men, with the aid of several persons working on the US side of the border, bought and sold at least $34 million since February of this year, illegally retaining a profit of 30 pesos for each dollar, or more than $4 million.

The newspaper further described specific details of the scheme.

By this point, however, my father had used the power of the Mexican press to put forward his own version of the story. In an open letter that more than one Tijuana newspaper graciously published, Jefe claimed that the whole investigation was a product of government corruption. That was his story, and he was sticking to it. So were my grandmother and mother, out of fear more than anything else.

Over the years, Ama had come to see my father for who he was. But Don Fernando had remained the stately, even-keeled patriarch of the family. For him to be in jail, and for the volatile man of the family to now be in charge, was beyond destabilizing. The reversal took her breath away. She and Abuela had held on to the bullshit narrative for a long time, but now there was no denying the truth about what their husbands' work was really all about.

The third, and by far most fun, camp was made up of Nando and me. We made the most of our stay at The Breakers. While my dad was holed up in the room, we played tennis on clay courts, went swimming in the cold Atlantic, and dined like kings. The hotel's key lime pie was so good that my mother asked to meet the chef, who invited her back into the kitchen to learn the recipe. (She'd done the same thing during a previous trip to Italy—more specifically, in the airport in Rome on our way back home. Before our flight, we stopped for a bowl of pasta with a basic red sauce that blew us away. She asked to meet the cook and took the recipe back to San Diego, where she used it to make jars of sauce that became the favorite centerpiece for Christmas baskets for family and friends.) As far as I was concerned, being on the lam was rad. Then, about a week after we arrived at The Breakers, we unexpectedly had to leave there too.

"We can't stay here," was all Jefe said. Spooked by something—he would not say what—Dad went out and got a 1980s burgundy van with wood side paneling, a balloon top, four captain's chairs, a bench seat in the back that turned into a bed, and the amenity that I was most excited about: a mini TV. We were all excited about the TV. None of us had ever seen one inside a car, and we had no idea how it worked. (It turns out the technology, whatever it was, left a lot to be desired.)

Once The Breakers' staff had packed all our stuff into the van, my father wanted to be on the road, moving as much as possible, and that meant staying in a string of motels.

"We're just staying here overnight," he said when we rolled into the first motel of our trip. We stayed only one night in each motel, but at the first one, my dad made the rookie mistake of unpacking the van. The next morning, it was a shit show getting it all back in.

His face red with exertion as he tried to cram my abuela's huge suitcase into a spot it was never going to fit, he barked, "Fuck this! When we get to a big hotel, you can open up your suitcases. Until then, you have your little bags for the motels because I'm not loading this shit up every goddamn time."

We made our way up the Eastern Seaboard, moving from motel to motel. It was an awful scene. Dad would pay cash for rooms next to one another—always on the first floor where he could keep an eye on the van out front and watch for any suspicious types. It wasn't enough that the rooms were side by side; they also had to be connected. If they weren't, we would leave to go find another motel. The next morning, we would be out and on the road again, the van already conveniently packed. By our fourth motel, Ama and Abuela were mocking my dad: "Which shitty motel are you taking us to now? Motel 6?"

Nando and I still found a way to have fun. We had played golf while at The Breakers, even though neither my uncle nor I was very good. Nando's best friend, Toby, who was a champion golfer in Tijuana, had previously brought golf balls out to the ranch for us to hit into the ocean. I loved hitting golf balls with Toby, who'd even taken me out golfing a couple of times.

Although I never got serious about the sport, when we stopped in Jacksonville, I begged my uncle to take me to Sawgrass. I knew the course from watching the Players Championship on TV. The best players in the world competed at Sawgrass in Ponte Vedra, where the seventeenth hole, known as Island Green, is famous because you have to hit the ball into a hole on a green surrounded by water. I think I lost eight balls in the water playing that hole, but I didn't care. I had a great time. Plus, how many kids can say they've played Sawgrass?

A round of golf with Nando became my treat whenever we could arrange it at one of our stops. Once, while we were on the fairway at one course, we heard an odd foghorn sound that went off three times. The sound is meant to warn golfers of lightning storms and signal for them to get off the course. But Nando and I had no clue what it meant until someone from the club came careening toward us in a golf cart. "Guys," he said. "Didn't you hear the siren?"

"Yes, but what does it mean?" my uncle said.

"It means lightning is coming, and you two are standing out here holding steel rods in your hands."

Got it. After we'd hightailed it off the course, Nando and I had a good laugh over that one.

As much fun as playing golf on an internationally renowned course was, though, living cheek by jowl with one another soon got on all of our nerves. Every day was an emotional roller coaster that revved up with Dad's first call to Germán on the West Coast. *What's going on? What happened yesterday? What do we think they're going to do today?* My father had a litany of questions for Germán, then Alfredo, then Angelo, and finally Lupita. None of their answers ever completely satisfied him. This left him grumpy as hell and the rest of us on edge.

The close quarters on the motel route didn't do much to improve our moods. My mom and Abuela were used to their beautiful homes and to spacious and well-staffed hotels—not to tiny rooms with fluorescent lighting, industrial carpeting, and polyester-blend bedspreads.

"We can't live like this until my father is out," Ama seethed. "We need to find a home base for a little while." But Jefe was in charge now, and this meant that we all had to do what Jefe wanted.

Even Abuela got so pissed off at us one night that she wound up sleeping in the van. It began when my mother asked if she could help with the driving, because my father had insisted on doing all of it up until then.

"Well, we know who *can't* do any of the driving: Ama," Nando said about his own mother from the middle seat. "She's so bad, she ran someone over." We all laughed, even Jefe. The only person who didn't think my uncle's joke was so funny was Abuela. *"Cabrones!"* she said, telling us to stick it where the sun doesn't shine. *"Vayanse a la chingada."*

My uncle was famous for getting under people's skin, and he succeeded with Abuela. She would have none of his hazing, nor would she put up with us laughing our asses off. "I'm going to the van," she said. My father and uncle bet she would come back in by midnight, but my grandmother stood her ground and slept in the van all night.

We all had something that got on our nerves eventually. For me, it was the TV that I had, at first, thought was so cool. Unfortunately, it only worked when the van was stopped and near a strong antenna signal. When we were moving, the only thing that was visible on that goddamn TV was a blurry line. If the point of this TV had been to entertain us while we were driving, it did not serve its purpose. The entire trip, my family had to hear me say, "This TV is horrible" four, five, or six times a day.

About a month after Abuelo's arrest, Jefe relented on the issue of the motel living for a couple of nights when we got into Charleston. Ama loved anything with "Southern charm," and Charleston was full of it. We stayed in a historic hotel, even though historic hotels are not known for their efficiency, size of rooms, or comfort. My mom was in seventh heaven. My dad, on the other hand, hated it. For him, the newer a place was, the better. He couldn't wait to get the hell out of there.

While laying low, the family got testy. Close quarters weren't the real problem. The fact that my grandfather was sitting in a Mexican federal prison where he had no protection was the real source of everyone's stress. My father and mother hid this fact from my grandmother, but the guards were roughing up my grandfather pretty badly. There was no possibility of getting him out on bail, because in Mexico's criminal justice system, a person is guilty until proven innocent. He was interrogated, but—determined to protect his family—he held the line and didn't divulge any details about Dólares Controlados.

The first order of business for everyone's safety was getting Don Fernando out of the federal penitentiary and into the Tijuana jail, where the warden was in my family's pocket. In addition to hiring lawyers, my dad was bribing officials left and right to get the federal government off his father-in-law's ass.

A week or so after we hit Charleston, we arrived in New York. Driving into Manhattan was its own adventure. In California we drive fast, but there's room to drive fast. In New York, there's no room, but people drive fast anyway. And the honking! If you're not honking in New York, you're not driving. In the burgundy van, cars aggressively darting in and out of lanes all around us, my dad was doing everything in his power to drive defensively. He was used to driving his sleek sedans, which he could easily weave in and out of traffic. Now he was behind the wheel of a big, clumsy van that had no pickup. As we lumbered along, other cars coming at us from every direction, I could see his level of frustration quickly rising. Finally, he exploded.

"Fuck this place!" he said, hitting the gas. He made a decision: "I'm driving like I'm in Naples!"

The drivers in Naples are just as aggressive as the ones in New York City, if not more so. From that point on, Jefe drove the van like a bat out of hell. Over the bridge, he went one hundred miles per hour, two inches from the car in front of us, before swerving into the slow lane to pass it. Once we made it off the highway and into Manhattan, the city streets didn't slow him down any. He followed an ambulance through a few red lights and drove over a curb while the rest of us held on for dear life.

My dad didn't care that his entire family were passengers in this speeding van. He was in the zone. The race-car-driver past of his youth came rushing back in one hair-raising drive. Even after we came to a screeching halt in front of the Plaza, where we'd be staying, and the rest of us had released our death grips from our armrests, Jefe still had a barely perceptible smile on his face. Up until that moment, he had been buried in work, stress, and cautiousness. New York traffic had allowed him to get his aggression out through driving, providing him with a brief escape.

During our weeklong stay in Manhattan, Jefe had more to smile about than cutting off a few New York City drivers, because it was at this point that the situation finally began to turn. When Jefe learned that a certain judge had indicated he was receptive to a bribe, his confidence that Abuelo's situation would soon improve increased by a lot.

The successful takedown of my grandfather and dad hinged on the authorities locating the actual customs seal that Abuelo and Jefe had used in the scam. The stamping machine, which was used (sometimes falsely) to verify that trucks with merchandise had crossed the border, was supposed to be kept safely in the Mexican government customs office. But Abuelo kept a customs seal, which he was not supposed to have, at his customs brokerage office. Obtaining and maintaining possession of that seal, which he'd done by regularly delivering cash to customs officials, was an extremely illegal act. The only way to prove the charges that he had falsified government documents using the seal was to find it.

The federal authorities had a good feeling that the seal had been in my grandfather's possession before his arrest—and it had been. They obtained a search warrant for the customshouse, but they were unable to find the smoking gun. Back at the federal prison, my grandfather still hadn't broken, despite the beatings that were intended to get him to talk. Weeks had passed without the authorities getting any closer to the evidence they needed for a conviction, and the judges my father had bribed were pressuring them to move the old man. Days after we arrived in New York, the Mexican government was forced to relent.

Getting Abuelo transferred to the Tijuana jail was a huge win.

"*Gracias a Dios!*" cried Abuela, throwing her hands up in the air. Ama was quiet but exhaled a big breath.

The warden in Tijuana, having been greatly enriched by my father, welcomed my grandfather with open arms, and we all breathed a sigh of relief. That was the moment our journey shifted speed and direction. After spending about a week at the Plaza, we left New York and headed back south. My dad picked up the pace, taking bigger chunks of the Eastern Seaboard at a single stretch. With momentum on his and Abuelo's side, he felt he needed to quickly get closer to home.

In Sea Island, Georgia, we had our first call with my grandfather. We all took turns getting on the phone, my dad going first. I don't know what was said between the two men, because my father had his conversation in the other room, but I can guarantee that he hammered my grandfather over the fact that he hadn't crossed the border as he'd been instructed. My father was the type of man who didn't let things go, even when everyone already understood what had happened. Knowing how my father operated, I believe that, in every phone call we had with my grandfather in jail from then on, he drilled Don Fernando over the fact that he'd seriously fucked up by not listening to him.

What I can't imagine is what it must have been like for my grandfather to have to take that shit from my father. Ultimately, if my dad hadn't sold him on the Dólares Controlados con, my grandfather—and the rest of our family—would not have been in this situation. This outcome was the result of pursuing fast money. Yet my grandfather knew that he was at fault for having partnered with El Italiano. He felt stupid. Why hadn't he stayed true to his own beliefs instead of sinking down to the corrupt level of his son-in-law?

He also knew that if Ama had listened to him, divorced the man, and let him adopt me, we all would have had a very different life. Yes, there would have been long days of hard work at the customshouse, and no, we would not have had all the flashy jewels, cars, mansions, Italian suits, and trips to Vegas. But he could have provided his grandson with a solid upbringing, free from worry and filled with family joy. What more could a boy want than riding horses on a ranch and the peace of mind that came with knowing he was safe and loved?

Despite the resentment both men felt, however, my father and grandfather knew they needed to work together to get our family out of our situation.

"Okay, let's get your wife on the phone," my father said loudly from the other room. Then he walked into the room where the rest of us were huddled and handed the receiver to Abuela.

As soon as she heard her husband's voice, my grandmother began to sob.

"*Estás bien mi amor?* Are you okay?" she said, repeating the same phrase over and over, not letting my grandfather answer.

Eventually, Abuelo got a word in and reassured her that he was all right. My grandmother accepted the lie, knowing it was a lie. We all knew as we took turns talking to him. I went last. My mom coached me before I got on the line.

"Tell him what you did yesterday with your uncle. Tell him about the tennis and the golf," she said. Hearing that his grandson and son were with one another, trying to have the best time they could under awful circumstances, would be a bright spot.

"*Me da mucho gusto, Pichito,*" he said when I was able to tell him.

At least we ended the phone call on a good note. For Abuelo, I was always the good note.

CHAPTER 11

BACK IN BUSINESS

The entire time we were on the road, Ama made sure that I stayed in regular touch with my best friend, Will Beamer. My phone calls with Beamer—which my mom orchestrated behind the scenes so that their occurrences happened seamlessly, just as she did with everything in my life, even while we were on the lam—made me feel like I was back home.

My best friend knew exactly what was going on with my family. After the *L.A. Times* article appeared, everyone at home knew why I wasn't at school. Jefe worried so much about the conversations he had with the managers of the foreign exchange that he'd designated a random public phone in San Diego for Lupita, Angelo, or Alfredo to answer when it rang. But he was okay with me calling Beamer, because the Mexican government intelligence wasn't sophisticated enough to know about my circle of friends.

Will didn't ask me anything about life as a wanted criminal. Instead, we talked about the random stuff that was of interest to a pair of thirteen-year-old boys. We discussed who in our group of friends was a bonehead, who had crushes on which girls, and, of course, we talked about sports.

"Dude, are you going to play football? Because I am," Beamer said over the summer while I traveled between New Orleans and Texas.

In New Orleans, Mom and I had had a lot of fun eating beignets and taking a voodoo tour, but I was ready to go home and return to my life. I was excited to be a freshman and start the school year or, more specifically, play high school sports. I was a terrible student but a great athlete. Starting in second grade, I had frequently looked out the classroom window at the athletic field when I should have been paying attention in class. I just couldn't wait to get outside and play. I picked up every sport quickly, roller hockey at Francis W. Parker's lower school or baseball in middle school. Now I was eager to join sports teams at Francis W. Parker's high school. I absolutely loved competing.

I asked Ama if she thought it would be possible for me to try out for football. As I thought about starting my freshman year of high school in the fall of 1985, joining the football team with Beamer seemed vital. Would we make it back home in time for the start of school? "I don't know, honey," said my mother, who never lied to me.

After getting the okay from my father, she phoned Mrs. Beamer. It couldn't have been an easy call for my mother, who was a pillar of the community at Francis W. Parker. The school meant the world to her. Through hosting events, attending field trips, and making significant donations, Ama had worked hard to give our family the appearance of propriety. As far as anyone else had known, the La Grecas were a prominent, upstanding, lawful family—with a shit ton of money. But by the time my mom called Mrs. Beamer, however, the *L.A. Times* had reported on my grandfather's arrest, and the news of our troubles had surely circulated around San Diego.

"Sharon, everything looks like it's going to be back to normal, and Pietro wants to play foot—"

Even before my mom got the words out, Mrs. Beamer said, "Send him to me. I'll take care of him."

Despite the danger to her own family, which she was keenly aware of, Mrs. Beamer didn't think twice about taking me in. I'll never forget her generosity and kindness.

Germán drove to Arizona, where we had gone after Texas, to pick me up and drive me straight to the Beamers' house in Mission Hills the Sunday before the first football practice. After three months of running from the law, of being around my father night and day, and of worrying about my abuelo, at last all the tension left my body. After Germán had dropped me off at the main driveway, I walked around back, toward the pool, and entered the house through the back door that led to the kitchen. Mrs. Beamer was there, preparing dinner.

"Hi, Pietro!" she said warmly. "How are you? Will's upstairs waiting for you."

This was a routine I had followed a million times before, and it immediately catapulted me to normalcy. I ran upstairs, where I found Beamer.

"What's up, dude?" he asked as if nothing had happened and no time had passed. Physically and emotionally exhausted, I dropped my bags, grateful for the familiar welcome.

Although the Beamers had three boys, their household was a calming one—the kind of place where Taco Tuesday dinner actually happened on Tuesdays. Mr. Beamer, a respected estate lawyer, returned home every day at 6:00 p.m., at which point his wife would hand him a whiskey neat. Then she'd make a whiskey for herself—on the rocks—and they'd sit in the living room together and talk about their day before the entire family sat down for dinner.

After our first football practice, Beamer and I returned to his house, where we headed directly for Mrs. Beamer's sewing room. There had been no question that we would make the team. At Francis W. Parker, a small private school with only sixty-three kids in my graduating class, the football coach was so desperate for bodies, anyone who showed up to practice made the team.

The little back room had a small TV and video game set up, where we played *R.B.I. Baseball* while we waited for dinner. When it was Will's turn to play, he sat on the floor with his legs crossed, and I lay on the couch behind him. That day, I fell asleep while watching him play and stayed asleep for fourteen hours straight. Mrs. Beamer threw a blanket over me and let me sleep through dinner. I didn't wake up until the next morning.

The three weeks I spent with the Beamers were ones of blissful ignorance—both for me and the Beamers. None of us was aware that Jefe had dispatched three armed guards to circle the house while I was staying there. We never saw a single sign of them. They might as well have been hidden up in the trees.

It wouldn't have been the first time. Back when we still lived in Bonita, one security guard, Kevin, went to such great lengths to keep us safe that he even hid in the trash cans and trees when he patrolled the property. One evening during a night shift, he dropped out of a tree, surprising our maid, Consuelo, who had gone out to bring him coffee. She went *nuts*. For the next few days, Consuelo refused to take coffee out to anyone, no matter how much my mother asked.

"No, Señora," she said. "I'm not going out there anymore. They fall from the trees."

By the time I finally realized a security detail was trailing me, school had officially started up again. I was daydreaming in class, looking out the window, when I caught sight of Alex, the guard who drove me to school, walk by. I had never seen him do that before. *What the hell?* I thought to myself. Then it dawned on me: he was patrolling the school.

By that point, the federal judge in charge of my grandfather's case had ruled the case invalid. My grandfather might have been a fool for not crossing the border when my dad told him to. But he had remained savvy when it came to the customs seal. Abuelo never revealed its whereabouts or even acknowledged his possession of the seal to the police while he was in custody, and the authorities never found it. Without the crucial piece of evidence that would have linked the fraudulent government documents to my grandfather, the Mexican government couldn't prove its case against him.

It wasn't just a lack of a smoking gun that had gotten my grandfather out of jail, however. My dad had spent those months on the road leveraging the power he had with politicians and members of the press for whom he had laundered money. The articles that had been written in favor of Don Fernando had put public opinion firmly on his side, and the bribed judges, who had no interest in contradicting public perception, pushed for the release of my grandfather. The charges were also dropped against my dad, and a few days after Labor Day of 1985, both men were finally able to come home.

Following his transfer to the Tijuana jail, Abuelo had not only been out of danger, he'd also been back in business. From his cell—located conveniently in the warden's office and outfitted with a treadmill, TV, and desk—Don Fernando had continued to run the customshouse. Although his license was in limbo at the time, he'd returned to his old business of crossing trucks (carrying real merchandise this time) while in prison. He did this by paying a small-shop customs broker in southern Mexico to use their license while he worked on reinstating his own. In this way, Abuelo moved five hundred trucks a day across the border. Not bad work for a jailbird.

Still, after he got out of jail, he wasn't the same. I had expected my grandfather to look frail the first time I saw him after he got out of prison. He wasn't thin at all. If there was one thing Abuela always made sure of, it was that her husband was well fed. Once he got to the TJ jail, she oversaw the planning, preparation, and delivery of all his meals from thousands of miles away. Every single day, she called Teresita, who was still managing their home back in TJ, to ask what looked good in the market and find out how much Don Fernando had eaten the day before. Every single day, Germán delivered to the warden's office three meals that had been home-cooked by Teresita.

So, no, my grandfather was not thin when he was released from prison. He was, however, pale. Though he'd done much office work over his lifetime, my grandfather had always loved being outside in the sun with the horses on the weekends. His skin, which became a rich mahogany when he tanned, was now sallow. Abuelo's pallor took me for a curve, but I didn't discuss it with him. My grandfather never talked about prison after he got out: not what had happened to him inside or even the fact that he had been there at all.

While still in jail, my grandfather had declared that once he got out, he was never going to live in TJ again. But Don Fernando wasn't just done living in TJ. He also vowed that he would never again step foot in Mexico. And he never did. (My father wouldn't return for another twelve years.)

Abuelo's self-exile from his native country was driven partly by fear, partly by his wounded pride. As a respected businessman and member of society, he'd never imagined he could be betrayed by his peers and treated like a common criminal. The fact that this had happened had messed with his head.

Ama and Abuela knew how much Abuelo loved his home in TJ and how big a blow it was for him not to return to it. So the two women rented a house in the Coronado Cays only several doors down from our house and set about making sure he would feel at home there. My uncle also got a condo in Coronado. The whole family wanted to be close to one another for security.

With Lupita's help on the ground, Ama and Abuela brought objects from the house in TJ that were important to Don Fernando, like his bed, a favorite lounge chair, and even a silly key holder I had given my grandfather. Made in the shape of a butler who was holding a tray where a person could drop keys, it was a cheesy gift. But my grandfather loved it, so my grandmother made sure it was by the door in the Coronado rental. In the days before he was set to leave prison, she fretted over every detail, going so far as to make sure all his suits hung in the closet just so.

Abuelo didn't just need a new place to live, though. He also needed a new place of work. A new outlet mall had opened in the summer of 1985 on the opposite side of the border from his customshouse in Mexico. So, soon after arriving in Coronado, my grandfather negotiated a deal to rent out thirty thousand square feet of storage space in the back of the new mall.

This space, which he turned into an office, was less than twenty-five yards from the San Ysidro border and twenty-seven yards from his building. The buildings would have had to be connected to be any closer. The international border between them, however, was monitored at all times. Although distance-wise it would have taken only five minutes to walk from the customs building on the Mexico side to my grandfather's new office on the US side, his employees needed to allow about fifteen minutes of time in order to get through customs.

Abuelo himself was done crossing the border. He wouldn't even cross to return to the ranch and his horses, the place where he had once found release. A place that he had truly loved.

~

Our family was bleeding money. I could see it in my father's eyes. He had spent a ton on my grandfather's case and bribes. The customshouse brokerage had survived the Mexican financial crisis and my grandfather's personal one. But by the time my father returned from being a fugitive from the law, PL Exchange was fizzling out.

Its money-laundering operations had evaporated when the customs seal disappeared. Meanwhile, the brick-and-mortar foreign exchanges were experiencing a slower demise. Many factors would eventually lead my dad to downsize his empire from fourteen foreign exchanges along the US-Mexico border to just two in San Ysidro and one in Tijuana.

Changes in technology, infrastructure, and government economic policy all had begun to modernize the process for Mexicans who wanted to change their pesos into dollars within the country. People also were growing numb to the reality of devaluation, which had become a day-to-day part of life. The value of the peso had been in decline for so long that there was no longer a rush on the exchange. Whenever the currency's value dropped further, some people were willing to wait a few days to see if it went back up; others were simply resigned to the mess.

After my grandfather went to jail, the major US bank had stopped making loans to PL Exchange. If the established financial institution couldn't do business with the mob in the casino, it sure as hell couldn't give loans to money launderers in Mexico. But that was the least of my father's problems. My dad didn't need $50 million anymore. He didn't even need half of that because, by then, the Dunes had cut ties as well.

As Jefe wound down his business to three exchanges, and then eventually just one, less than $2 million in operating funds each month was plenty—and he had no problem securing that kind of loan from a smaller local bank that was willing to take that risk and not worried about its reputation. This was exactly what my father did for the next two years, until 1987 when he closed the last exchanges. With Jefe's approval and support, Alfredo and Lupita went out on their own and opened a mini exchange. Angelo, however, continued as my dad's right hand as Jefe figured out his next move.

Once again, now that his work had gone sideways, he was around the house way too much. When he wasn't going into the Jacuzzi, formulating a plan, or laying out in his Speedo, getting sun, he was on top of Ama and me, harping about my mom's weight and the Cs on my report card. The fact that his doctor had ordered him to quit smoking because of his high blood pressure didn't help his personality any. Every day, my mother and I wondered when he would switch out his Speedos for his Canali dress slacks and Brioni jackets. We needed him to get back to work.

Despite having been a wanted man, Jefe hadn't lost his friends in high places. López Portillo remained close to our family, so much so that while I was in high school, we hosted a big birthday party for him at our house. We pulled out all the stops for the black-tie event in honor of the former president. The guest list was a who's who of Mexican society, but it was Shu-Shu, our pet Vietnamese potbellied pig, that made the biggest splash. Nando, who always exchanged gag gifts with Ama at Christmas, had given her Shu-Shu, and now the guests were clamoring to meet her.

"You've got to bring down the potbellied pig!" one begged.

Ever the gracious host, my mom obliged, bringing the pig downstairs in her arms. Faced with a huge crowd, a nervous Shu-Shu peed all over my mother's gorgeous gown. Ama didn't get flustered. Without skipping a beat, she smiled at the president and said, "It looks like the pig had a little bit of an accident, which means you'll have to excuse me for a moment." She then walked up the stairs with the pig, changed outfits, and returned, to everyone's delight.

López Portillo's opulent birthday party fed both the president's ego and my father's. Journalists sipped champagne on the wraparound deck that overlooked the twinkling lights of San Diego and Coronado Bridge, actors and musicians gossiped around the self-playing piano, and cabinet members and other political figures traded favors over ceviche. The collective presence of all these people—eating, drinking, and laughing—was a clear symbol of the men's importance.

It is possible that none of the guests had more power than Garza, who was still a high-ranking government official in Mexico. Though he'd started out as the right hand of López Portillo, he had long surpassed the former president's influence and authority—that is, if those qualities are defined by who holds the secrets. From cabinet members to cab drivers, everyone in Mexico feared Garza. He wielded a particularly great amount of control over my father at this point, since he was the force behind Jefe's newest major income stream.

After the conclusion of the foreign exchanges in 1987, Garza had enlisted my father as the middleman in a pure shakedown scheme. It went like this: Garza identified a wealthy Mexican citizen who did not know that they were about to be audited. My dad's job was to approach this person, some weeks before they learned of their audit, and offer to solve their tax woes at a fraction of the cost of the impending heavy tax lien. The person would then either take Jefe up on his offer or tell him to get lost. But even if they at first told him to get lost, they would inevitably engage his help once the audit materialized. Either way, my father made the problem go away for a bribe that Garza split with him sixty-forty.

Garza knew my dad was the perfect man for the job. Jefe had a knack for always landing on his feet and never in jail. Despite the jam my dad had gotten into when the Dunes couldn't make its payment, he'd never screwed over or stolen from any of his clients. He defied the president only because he needed the money and nobody else would help him. Even then, he'd really only been fucking over the Mexican government. Yes, my father was a criminal a person could trust.

After the men partnered in the tax scheme—which went on for several years—our family went hand in hand with the Garzas. From the time I was a sophomore in high school until I was a freshman in college, our families used to have Puerto Nuevo lobster parties at our house and even travel together. I was very friendly with the Garza children, who were both younger than me. At one point, my mom and Garza's wife even got plastic surgery within one day of each other, so they could recuperate together.

They both had their nips and tucks done by the same plastic surgeon, Dr. Robert Singer. A renowned doctor, he was at the time considered the godfather of plastic surgery in San Diego, where people do not shy away from going under the knife for aesthetic purposes. My family knew Dr. Singer well.

The surgeon loved to dress well. But at five foot two, he could never find Brioni suits, like the kind my father favored, which fit Jefe properly. My dad, who had a contact at the Italian menswear company, said, "Let's get you measured, Doc. I'll get you your suits." Jefe hooked him up with a tailor and ten custom Brioni suits, delivered directly from Italy to La Jolla. To this day, Dr. Singer remembers my dad. Over the Christmas and Easter holidays, a flood of people from Mexico City would arrive in San Diego to go shopping and get their plastic surgery. Starting during the Dólares Controlados days, whenever my father had an important client or connection whose wife wanted plastic surgery, Dr. Singer would always put her at the front of the line.

There was no patient more important than Garza's wife, who, after her surgery, lay in a queen bed alongside my mother's in a five-bedroom La Jolla home that Dr. Singer had transformed into a private convalescing facility for patients who were willing to pay extra. When I went to visit my mom, I found two mummified women covered in ice packs, soaps playing in the background of their room, chatting and laughing like *comadres*.

There was on occasion some crossover between my dad's old business of laundering money and his new one of extorting it. That's what happened when he received a visit from one of his former tellers, Violeta, a beautiful woman who had married Benjamin Arellano Félix. Benjamin, who'd been arrested in 1982 with one hundred kilos of cocaine he'd smuggled over the San Ysidro border, was now running the Arellano-Félix Organization (AFO), otherwise known as the Tijuana Cartel. Known for trafficking cocaine, marijuana, heroin, and methamphetamine to the United States, it was at that time considered the most violent cartel in Mexico. If anyone encroached on Benjamin and his brother Ramon's Mexicali/Tijuana territory without cutting them in, the men had the interlopers assassinated to send a message.

Violeta had met Benjamin during PL Exchange's heyday, when he used to bring his money to be laundered. Now, she wanted to know if her old boss could help her husband, who was facing a tax fine in the millions. They had heard Jefe could do something about it.

My dad was up front with Violeta. "I don't know if I can fix this," he said. Garza led the charge on all the shakedowns; my dad just did what he was told. "He comes to me. I don't go to him," Dad told her. "I will go to him for you. But if he says no, I will tell you he said no." My father was no dummy; he didn't want to be shot and killed by Benjamin's people. He didn't want to refuse to help, but he didn't want to promise that he could deliver, either, when he wasn't sure that he could.

The only way to make sure no one got killed was to ensure that everyone involved made money—so that's exactly what my dad did. He and Garza earned $4 million from the AFO, their biggest payday so far.

The bribe was so big that it might have raised some kind of regulatory eyebrows if it was deposited in a bank account on either side of the border. Instead, Jefe bought him a Ferrari Testarossa and parked the present outside the $2 million house my father had just put in the Garzas' name.

CHAPTER 12

OFF TO THE RACES

My grandfather had long known the ranch and much of the surrounding sprawling property would eventually have to be developed. Since the time when he'd originally squatted on the land, the location had gone from being a desolate outpost to being prime real estate. The ranch was now smack-dab in the middle of Rosarito, which had grown from a small and sleepy beach town to a major spring break destination. Development was spreading south along the coast during the '80s. Only thirty minutes to the north, Tijuana had seen its own population nearly double throughout the decade, thanks to migration and urbanization. Its spillover population had contributed to Rosarito's transformation into a bustling new city.

The impetus to start on a development project on the ranch's land didn't come from market forces, however, but from my uncle. Nando, who was no longer employed at my father's money exchange and still averse to joining the family commercial brokerage, had begun agitating to develop the land.

In 1990, Abuelo gave his son his blessing. Don Fernando never went to Mexico anymore, which was probably why he was finally ready to let his beloved ranch get turned into a mall and housing. This involved dismantling the equestrian center and finding other pastures for the horses he no longer rode anyway. There was one major caveat to his agreement: Nando had to raise the money for the project on his own.

"You've got to secure the financing. Good luck," Abuelo said, knowing full well that his playboy son could never pull that off. My uncle—still young, fun, and a little crazy—had no money or business sense. Perhaps Abuelo didn't want to foot the bill for any of Nando's mistakes, or maybe he wanted to sabotage his son's efforts so he would have to come into the family business. Either way, my uncle wasn't getting a peso from my grandfather.

True to Nando's style, the plans for the future Plaza San Fernando were extravagant. Phase one of the development on my grandfather's property in Rosarito would be the shopping center that stood on *La Uno*, or more accurately, Federal 1, which was an extension of US Highway Route 101 that runs along the Pacific Coast. The plan was not to build a small strip mall like the ones that already dotted the San Ysidro border but rather a massive American-style shopping center with more than three hundred retail units. Behind the shopping center site, going east toward the mountains, a seventy-home development would also be built. Across the road from the shopping center, on the western side facing the Pacific Coast, Abuelo's ranch—soon to be home to a luxury hotel and resort—was surrounded by fifteen thousand feet of private beachfront.

Sure enough, Nando struggled to get the financing, just as Abuelo had expected. My uncle was surprised. He'd thought he was a big deal in TJ. Coming off the whole foreign-exchange scandal, my father had made sure through his work with the newspapers that my grandfather had the respect he deserved and that the rest of our family could still hold our heads up high. Nando had believed he didn't need his dad's money, but he ran into roadblocks everywhere he went for a loan.

He was about to be turned down at yet another bank when a loan officer said to him, "Wait. So you're La Greca's brother-in-law? Is he in on this deal?"

"No, he's not."

"Well, if he was, I think we'd probably make it happen."

My uncle hadn't been shrewd enough himself to come up with the idea to use my father to get the money. Once the other man planted it in his head, however, Nando didn't hesitate to approach his brother-in-law, whom he knew was on the hunt for new moneymaking opportunities. Now that he no longer had the constant influx of cash that the exchange had provided, Jefe needed a lot of irons in the fire in order to keep up with a lavish lifestyle that included a few Rolls-Royces and a $2.3 million home.

One of those irons involved a questionable rental arrangement. After closing the last of his money exchanges a few years earlier, my father had given Angelo and Alfredo his blessing for them to start their own small (and legit) exchange. He'd given his approval in part because he could make money off it. My grandfather, who had moved the customshouse brokerage office to San Ysidro, now rented out his old building in Tijuana, and my father had siphoned off a quarter of the first floor for Angelo and Alfredo's foreign exchange—pocketing not only the rent but also a percentage of their profits. Because they were indebted to my father, Angelo and Alfredo accepted the terms.

In addition to that revenue stream, Jefe was also still extorting money from wealthy Mexicans under Garza's auspices. But no matter how much money Dad made, it never seemed like quite enough. As much money as he was making, we were burning right through all of it.

That was part of the reason for Jefe's feverish excitement over his latest opportunity, which he believed could be his biggest score ever. "This is the *fuck-you* money," he told my mom and me. "The *we don't have to think about money anymore* kind of money."

My father had recently learned that the government contract to manage the racetrack and sports book in Juarez was up for bid. Juarez—on the border with Texas and the most dangerous city in all of Mexico—was entertaining multiple offers. Carlos Hank González—the crooked, politically connected titan of industry—appeared to be the front-runner. But Hector Guzman, a fixer out of Mexico City, put the bug in my dad's ear that the deal was still in play.

Hector and Jefe were two peas in a pod. Both hustlers who were always in search of a quick and easy buck, they had been trading scores and scams since the '70s. My dad's introduction to Garza had come through Hector, who now assured him that he had an inside line to the officials in charge of giving out the lucrative betting concession. Swinging for the fences, Jefe joined forces with Hector and two other men who had enough financial and political muscle to actually win it.

Jefe's obsession with the sports book wasn't just about money. Winning this contract was also part of my grandfather and father's constant battle to claim the title of patriarch. Money was the biggest weapon they used to fight this battle.

It still drove Abuelo nuts when my dad gave my grandmother jewelry in a cheap move to stoke jealousy between husband and wife. Abuela loved her jewels. The flashy baubles he lavished on her elevated my dad in her eyes so that the former beauty queen fawned over him, just as she would any benefactor. Seeing his own wife express her gratitude toward and admiration for that no-good son-in-law of his pissed off my grandfather to no end. That was the whole point of my father doing what he did.

Whenever both men were rolling in money, they tried to outdo one another in gifts. In my case, my grandfather and dad dueled for my affection with cars. Once I got my license at sixteen, my father bought me a Mercedes 500 SEL. Then, using the excuse that he didn't want me driving the Mercedes to the ranch (since the foreign car put a target on my back once I crossed the border into Mexico), Abuelo bought me a

Ford Bronco with the instruction to "ruin that car." I had so much fun following my grandfather's wishes, off-roading as fast as I could without a thought to scratching the paint job or wrecking the suspension, that my father decided he needed to buy me the best off-road car on the market: a Range Rover.

During Dólares Controlados, the men had called a truce so that they could work together. But the peace had ended with the foreign exchange, and Jefe and Abuelo had returned to being enemies. After prison, Abuelo was clearly weaker but still animated by his hate of El Italiano. My father, for his part, resented my grandfather more than ever before. If the old man had only listened, Jefe thought, then he wouldn't be without an empire and in need of money, after having spent a fortune to restore his and my grandfather's legal standing.

The tension that lay beneath every single one of their interactions was at play, big-time, when Nando approached my dad about partnering with him in the development of Plaza San Fernando. My father was thrilled by the prospect. Unlike the sports book, where being all in meant investing his own money, the ranch project offered Jefe a chance to profit from the bank's money. But that wasn't the only reason he was excited. Jefe was also going to get to demolish a place he had always hated—his father-in-law's ranch. Jefe's involvement in the project did bother Abuelo, but not for the reasons my dad thought. El Italiano had already stolen his daughter. Now, my grandfather feared, he was also taking his son.

This—and not the demise of the ranch—was what really upset my grandfather. He'd already vowed that he was never going to step foot in Mexico again. He would not miss the ranch.

My uncle and I, however, went there all the time. It was a great place to hold parties and to bring girls. Although the ranch now had about one-third the number of horses it once did, Nando and I had continued to be big riders—especially after we got into polo.

In 1988, his girlfriend at the time—a beautiful and wealthy Texan with big blonde hair—had introduced him to the rich man's sport. I was still in middle school when Mina invited Nando to Retama Polo Center, which was, at that time, with its sixteen fields and stables and approximately four hundred horses, one of the country's best facilities. Over the course of a week, Nando fell in love with the game. Upon his return home from Texas, he told me, "Screw this jumping shit; we're playing polo."

From that point on, we played one-on-one polo matches in Rosarito, kicking up dirt with our swinging mallets. Nando taught me how to use aggression to get the most out of a horse. He showed me how to pull on the bottom set of reins and mess around with the bit so that the horse got nice and pissed off. It was like riling up a team member before a game.

Although Abuelo had been skeptical about polo when we first started playing it at the ranch, after his release from prison, he dramatically changed his position and fully supported our interest in the game. Because he couldn't go back to Mexico, he'd given up on the ranch and his own riding. But he didn't give up on the activity for his son and grandson. His backing was no small thing, considering that polo is a costly sport.

My grandfather spared no expense, as my uncle and I entered into the world of competitive polo. We played at the Fairbanks Polo Club in Del Mar, California, where Don Fernando soon stabled a dozen or so horses. He also purchased a new home in Fairbanks Ranch, which wasn't just the swankiest gated community in all of Rancho Santa Fe. It was also far from Coronado. By then, he'd had enough of my father and was happy to move away from him.

I learned the game from some of the best polo players in the world, including the pros my grandfather hired to play with Nando and me. (In polo, each team has four players.) In one match we played during my first season, our team was awarded a penalty shot from midfield, which is 150 yards out.

"Hey, P," one of the pros said. "We got this game in the bag. Do you want to hit this one?"

"Fuck yeah!"

Despite my enthusiasm, at nineteen years old I had a handicap of minus two, the lowest ranking, indicating I was a new player, in a system that goes up to ten. Our pros, who each had a seven-goal handicap, could score a goal from half field about 50 percent of the time. According to the math, I had a snowball's chance in hell of making the shot. But—young, strong, and too green to know better—I flew one right between the uprights and scored the goal. The announcer shouted, "This guy is a minus two and it's his first season!" It was a thrilling moment.

Polo itself was having a moment in the '80s. Hollywood was into it. Actors and actresses from LA started to come down to San Diego to play in and watch celebrity tournaments. I played in one game with William Devane, who played the power-hungry Greg Sumner in *Knots Landing*. I got to meet Sylvester Stallone and once knocked Tony Robbins off his horse—by mistake. The fashion brand Polo by Ralph Lauren was also huge. About thirty Polo shirts in every color hung in my closet, thanks to the trips to Neiman Marcus I took with Abuela and Ama.

My grandfather ended up loving polo every bit as much as Nando and I did. Attending the matches allowed him to sublimate his thwarted love for the ranch into a new pastime that combined his passion for horses, pomp, and partying. For him, the highlight of the time we spent playing polo may have been the time we played with royalty.

On a family trip to Europe in the summer of '91, Nando set up a practice match at Guards Polo Club, Europe's largest polo club, located in the Great Park at Windsor, five miles south of Windsor Castle. Leaving my grandmother, mom, and dad to spend a day shopping in

London, Abuelo accompanied my uncle and me in a private car to the polo facilities.

While we were mounting up, the stable hand helping me out with the horses said, "You'll be going up against Charles today, you know?"

"Charles who?"

"Prince Charles."

"Get out of here!"

Prince Charles, twenty-three years my senior, was a great player, and because he was playing forward and I was a defenseman, we were up against one another the entire match.

All eight of us on the field had a blast. As we were hanging out and chatting after the game, the prince himself invited us to watch his team play in a regular match the next day. Naturally, we RSVP'd yes for our entire family on the spot.

Having spent a couple of hours stick-and-balling with a real-life member of the House of Windsor, Abuelo, Nando, and I decided not to go right back to the hotel, where everyone else was waiting, but to a pub for a drink or two. We boys were having such a good time going over every detail of the epic day, and were so busy getting wasted on pints, that we blew off dinner. My grandfather was smiling from ear to ear. He couldn't have been happier than he was in that moment, talking about horses with his grandson and his son.

When we returned to the hotel around eleven o'clock at night, the rest of our family was beyond pissed off. Even my mother, who never got angry with me, was furious. After they finished chewing us out, Abuelo dropped the news on them. "Well, would you still be mad at us if I told you the boys played polo today with Prince Charles?" He said this as if it were the most normal thing in the world. "And he's invited us all to be his personal guests at his match tomorrow?" My mother and grandmother—both big Princess Diana fans—didn't say a word. Instead, they went straight to their rooms to find something to wear.

The next day, we went off to the Guards Polo Club as if we were about to be knighted. The event, held on a stadium field, did not disappoint. Prince Charles galloped regally on the field while Princess Di cheered demurely from the stands. At least, that's what my mother told me afterward. I was too busy watching the action on the field to pay any attention to the fans—even the royal ones.

But the real highlight, at least for my family, came at halftime. After the third chukker—or period—there is a tradition of divot stomping. That's where the match's spectators take to the field to flatten out hunks of the pitch churned up by the hooves and mallets. Champagne in hand, men and women revel in pressing the grass back down with the soles of their fancy footwear.

The Guards Polo Club had been founded by Prince Philip and named after a division of the British Army, so it was fitting that during halftime, a marching band appeared to play military-esque music. From the first crash of the cymbals, Abuelo was up off his seat. The man loved a marching band like no one else. All those equestrian events he'd held at the ranch had been accompanied by canned marching band music blaring through speakers. Now *this* was the real thing.

Abuelo grabbed my grandmother by the hand and pulled her onto the grass, where he began marching in rhythm directly behind the last line of musicians. He followed the band as it wound its way around the field. Behind him, he dragged my poor abuela, whose pencil skirt didn't allow for large strides and whose four-and-a-half-inch heels sank into the Windsor polo field. Abuelo didn't stop until the announcer—in his most posh and polite voice—said, "Will the gentleman and lady walking behind the marching band please return to your seats, as it's time to resume the match."

I thought my grandmother was going to die of embarrassment. As much makeup as my grandmother wore, you could see her face turn red under all that foundation. Not my grandfather, though. He thought he was a part of the goddamn band. We teased him about it mercilessly for the rest of the vacation and beyond. He didn't care. He'd had the time of his life that day.

"I marched at Windsor Castle behind a band," he said. "I could give two fucks what you guys think."

~

Ten days after Nando approached my father about joining him in the San Fernando housing, hotel, and shopping center development, Jefe secured a $30 million loan to finance the project.

Of course, my dad never did a deal without skimming a little something off the top for himself. The actual projected cost of the project was $20 million; the extra $10 million was to be split among the banking officials, my dad, and Nando—whose taste for the good life was unparalleled.

Nando found excess to be a source of excitement. Even when it came to women, my uncle—who had no trouble attracting the ladies, thanks to his good looks and profligate ways—could never get enough. He was into prostitutes in a big way, and he hired them at home, on vacation—pretty much wherever he went.

When, as a little kid, I was sent to wake him up while we were on a family vacation, I naively thought he'd used his charm to get the two women asleep in his hotel room into bed. Nando happily took on the role of older brother in schooling me about sex. When I was in sixth grade and had just hit puberty, he taught me what jerking off was all about, showing me my first *Playboy* from his stash under the sink in his bathroom. He also paid for me to lose my virginity. The night before my tenth-grade homecoming, my uncle told me to meet him at the Westgate Hotel downtown. "P, I've got a surprise for you," he said. The "surprise" turned out to be four call girls waiting for me in a suite. I was so scared, but I spent about three minutes with one of the women, who unceremoniously popped my cherry.

Nando gave me everything he wanted for himself—like the epic after-prom party he threw for me at the San Diego Marriott's two-floor presidential suite, which he filled with beer and other booze. I had a lot to celebrate. I was headed off to San Diego State in the fall on a baseball scholarship.

I'd come to the sport relatively late. My parents never signed me up for Little League. My mom didn't have a clue that other mothers were doing this for their sons, and my dad was not a sports guy. He didn't even watch sports—except for big boxing events with great heavyweights like Muhammad Ali and, every four years, the World Cup (especially if Italy made the finals). While my other friends, like Beamer and Trevor, played organized sports on the weekends, I had been getting shipped out to the ranch in Rosarito.

In seventh grade, however, Dave Glassey, Francis W. Parker's baseball coach and one of the best in San Diego, got me playing the quintessential American pastime. My freshman year, our team won the California Interscholastic Federation (CIF) Championship when Beamer, our pitcher, threw a great game to me, the catcher. We would go on to bring four league titles and three CIF Championship trophies home to Coach Glassey over my four years of high school.

My mom might not have known anything about baseball before, but once I started playing, she loved to come to my games. My biggest fan, she didn't miss a single one. Once she came late to a game and was upset that she'd missed the top of the first inning, when I'd hit a hanging curveball out of the park. Three innings later, when I was up to bat again, another Francis W. Parker parent yelled, "Hey, Pi, your mom missed the first homer! Hit another one!" I did, and everyone, especially Ama, went wild.

Senior year, I was offered scholarships to play baseball at more than five Division I universities throughout the US, including San Diego State University. Ama didn't want her only child, her little baby, going away to a university. Even colleges in Los Angeles, less than three hours away from San Diego, were too far for her. She didn't have the courage to let me go, and I didn't have the heart or desire to leave her.

The decision to stay home for college turned out to be a fraught one, however. This began the day I came home from practice and my parents sat me down to relay the news that my mother had breast cancer.

"It's not a big deal," Ama said. "They're just going to take a little bit off and do some light radiation. It's nothing really to worry about. We caught it early."

My mother was adamant that she was going to keep her breast intact. Her breasts were a big deal to her. My dad liked them, and she thought they were the sexiest part of her body. The doctor thought a lumpectomy, followed by a course of radiation and chemo, would be fine. But the surgery and treatment turned out to be much harder than she expected.

Abuela, a breast cancer survivor who'd had a double mastectomy, was torn up by guilt because she'd passed the disease down to her daughter. My grandmother never left Ama's side as she underwent treatment in Los Angeles at UCLA Medical Center. My father rented a place right off Wilshire Boulevard where he, my grandmother, and uncle stayed with my mother during the week. Abuelo, however, was not part of my mom's support network. Still traumatized by his own wife's battle with the cancer, our family rock was unable to watch his daughter go through the same illness. He made up excuses: too much work, my grandmother was there, he would just be in the way. But it disappointed and saddened my mother that he didn't come visit with the rest of us after her surgery.

I was going through my own struggles. My mom and best friend in the whole world was battling cancer. At the same time, I was an eighteen-year-old college freshman who wanted to have fun. Released from my small, conservative private school, I dove headlong into the heady social life of a Southern California undergrad. A baseball player who drove a Mercedes and threw parties at his family's empty house overlooking Coronado Bay? Yeah, you could say I was pretty popular. My parents were busy with my mom's treatments, procedures, and test results, so they had no knowledge of how I was doing in school, which was not good. While academics had never been my strong suit, now I was a complete dumb shit. I never went to class, so I shouldn't have been surprised when I got four Fs my first semester. I did everything I could during my second semester to stay in school and improve my grades (they couldn't get worse), but the effort wasn't enough to keep me in.

By the time my mom received a clean bill of health, I had been expelled from San Diego State.

CHAPTER 13

OTHER PEOPLE'S MONEY

The beautiful flight attendant came through first class one more time to see if there was anything we needed before we touched down in Singapore, where we had a connecting flight to Kuala Lumpur. Never one to leave an offer on the table—especially not while on Singapore Airlines, then the best airline in the world—Nando ordered one more champagne and a hot towel.

The same summer we traveled to England and played against Prince Charles, my uncle and I headed to Malaysia after one of the country's princes invited us to play polo. We'd come a long way since our days of one-on-one in dusty Rosarito, and we had upped our game all the way to high-goal polo, the most competitive level in the sport.

Nando had made a huge financial investment to get two ten-goalers to play with us at the Empire Polo Club, the Palm Springs club that attracted some of the world's wealthiest players. That's where we met the Malaysian prince. The tournament boasted the likes of Southeast Asian princes and the scion of the General Electric company: a billion-dollar industrial company that at the time was Britain's largest private employer.

Nando and I joined Jay Haagen, whose family owned the Empire Polo Club, and a Chilean pro to represent America in a tournament against Australia, Britain, Argentina, and other polo-playing countries. The four of us arrived in Malaysia with little but our clothes, pads, helmets, and boots. The royal family of Pahang hosting the games had agreed to provide everything else—including our horses. One of nine royal families, which take turns ascending the throne of Malaysia's constitutional monarchy, theirs had a large state in the country's east coast as their domain. There, we were put up in an opulent resort on the water where the polo players were the only guests.

Then, as if renting out an entire hotel hadn't been enough to signal their enormous wealth, the Malaysian royals competing in the tournament arrived via a helicopter that landed on the beach! When it came time to play a couple of practice matches, they hopped back in their chopper while the rest of us drove to the fields, accompanied by a police motorcycle escort. The policeman on the motorcycle next to our car was so close, I could have touched him if I had put my hand out the window. So it was with horror that I watched when he flew off his bike. I didn't know why he crashed—or even if he was okay—because our procession did not fucking stop. No one even braked. Our driver and the motorcade just kept going, like the person did not matter.

That wasn't the only shocking thing that happened on that trip. Not by a long shot. Our team didn't do well in the tournament, and one day we found ourselves playing against Australia in a consolation match for last place. We tied after six chukkers played out on a gruelingly humid 105-degree day, and the players on both teams were good with that. But there was one person who wasn't.

On one side of the polo fields, across from the spectator stands, there was an odd piece of train track whose ends led nowhere. Parked on the bit of track was a train engine, a main car, and caboose. We players had just started to take off our equipment when a small man came out of the caboose and sprinted to the officiating table. He had his arms raised, and he was yelling as if there were an emergency. He spent no more than a minute or two talking to the officials before he ran back to the caboose. Next, the players were summoned to the scoring table, where we were instructed to finish the match in overtime. We were incredulous.

"We've tied. It's for last place," I said. "Who cares?"

"The king cares," an official said, "which means you care."

It turned out, one of the country's kings—who was also the father of the princes we had played against and lost to earlier in the tournament—was watching from the train that was parked on the side of the field. The man who had run from the train car to the scoring table was his representative, and he'd run out to express the king's displeasure at the prospect of a tie.

As the captain of our team, I made the Australian team's captain an offer he couldn't refuse. Overtime started with the traditional throwing in of the ball between the two teams lined up on either side. When the ball came toward our goal, my job as the defenseman was supposed to drive it out. Instead, I would miss the ball on purpose, and the Australian team would then take it in for a goal. That's exactly what happened. Within a minute of overtime starting, the other team scored and won the game. The king was happy, and so were we—once we got out of that godforsaken heat.

No one was surprised that the three Malaysian teams—each with its own member of the royal family—won first, second, and third place in the tournament. It was what it was. We had fun playing our matches, and at the postgame ball, the king apparently enjoyed the company of the Latin polo players so much, he insisted we all join him in Kuala Lumpur. And there were a lot of us, since most of the teams had at least one Latin pro playing with them. South Americans—in particular, Argentinians—are known as the best polo players in the world. Each prince had three professionals, all from South America, on their teams. When we were at the resort earlier in the trip, you might as well have spoken Spanish because it was practically all Latins. We were in, but we told him we needed to buy tickets for a flight to the capital.

"No," the king declared. "You will fly with me."

I don't know what the other guys were expecting, but I thought flying with royalty would mean that we'd take a Malaysia Airlines plane that had been tricked out and turned into a private jet. Instead, we all were loaded into a C-130 cargo plane with no windows—royalty included. It was like traveling by bumpy flying box. We couldn't tell if we were going up or down. Needless to say, it was not the most joyous flight in the world.

After we were finally down on the earth, we consoled ourselves that we were about to have the night of our lives. But instead of heading to one of the towering luxury hotels of downtown Kuala Lumpur, we soon found ourselves taken *outside* the city to a massive old-school-style villa on a hill that overlooked the twinkling lights of the city. We were young and wanted to experience a scene, but not the scene we got. There was no one more pissed than my uncle to find himself surrounded by forty other guys in suits and ties. (The king had provided suits to those who didn't pack them.) A night without women was no night at all for Nando, who stared daggers at me for a half hour or so until the large doors to the grand ballroom opened and in walked a crowd of paid escorts.

I didn't see my uncle again until the next morning, when I assumed my usual task of waking him up. We had to catch a flight to Hong Kong, where we would stay for a night before flying home to San Diego. I was exhausted from the whirlwind of excess and competition, but Nando wasn't ready to slow down yet. I watched as he called up the son of the head of the General Electric company. The Brit we had competed against in the tournament had mentioned that he had a place in Hong Kong. Nando wanted to know if he was in town. The man wasn't, but he said "his team"—his staff in the city—was. He told us someone would pick us up from the airport and make sure we were taken care of.

The man was true to his word. We were met by a six-foot-three driver who—given his large size, gruff demeanor, the black Ray-Bans he wore even at night, and his *gun*—could have easily doubled as a hit man. He shepherded us to an unforgettable dinner at a restaurant with a sweeping view of the Hong Kong bay. When we were done with our meal, he delivered us to a nondescript door in a dark alley where—just like in the movies—someone slid open a small window to reveal a peephole. The driver said a password under his breath so we couldn't hear, and the door swung open to reveal a swanky club filled with quiet corners, gambling tables, and beautiful women.

Next morning, it fell on me again to rouse Nando.

"We got to go, dude," I said, shoving him. "It's over. We're going back home."

"How'd we do last night?" he asked when he finally opened his eyes. "Did we spend it all?"

Before the trip, Nando had put me in charge of the $30,000 in cash we had brought. We only spent $4,000 before arriving in Hong Kong, because nearly everything had been covered by our Malaysian hosts. But last night had been a doozy.

"We blew through about $14,000," I said, shaking my head.

Nando grinned and winked at me.

"We came back with money, though."

My uncle wasn't just being cute. The fact that we were returning with some money left over—and were not in debt—was a miracle.

Thanks to the level of polo we had been playing for the last year, we were running in circles we had no business being in. I'm talking about stupid levels of wealth. The shit I saw when we played high-goal polo, I've never seen before—or again—in my life. And it wasn't like I'd grown up in shabby circles. Polo is a sport that requires boatloads of money for participants to play at the most competitive level, and that was the only level my uncle wanted to be part of. Not only did our family team now keep sixteen horses at the Fairbanks polo facilities, but we also hired two ten-handicappers to play on our teams. There are only about a dozen professional polo players with a ten handicap in the world at any given time, so that gives you an idea of how much we were spending on these guys.

As well-off as our family was, we didn't have the money of a prince of Malaysia or a prince of Wales. But Nando was acting like we did—by using the bank loan for Plaza San Fernando as if it were his personal checking account.

I didn't realize it at the time. I thought there was plenty of money to go around. But by 1991, my uncle's reckless spending had begun to put the whole development in jeopardy. He was now draining the $20 million from the original $30 million loan that had been designated for the actual construction, and he was doing so at an alarming rate. My uncle, who had a huge lust for life, was a ton of fun. And polo, and its world, was a source of great fun for him. But polo wasn't the problem. It was a symptom. The problem was that he never knew when to quit.

By the time I graduated from high school, I had assumed the role of caretaker. Wherever and whenever I could, I protected my uncle from himself, just as I did when I took charge of our cash during our trip to Malaysia. Since I'd been expelled from college, I had grown up even further. Getting kicked out of school had been a rude awakening. But it was going to work for my grandfather that really matured me.

With companies like the oil giant Petróleos Mexicanos (PEMEX) and the grocery store chain Calimax as its clients, the customshouse was still going strong, even if Abuelo was starting to fade. He was looking for a successor. Nando didn't have it in him; he didn't want to do the job. But my grandfather knew pretty quickly after I started to work for him that he and I were cut from the same cloth.

After getting expelled from San Diego State, I'd begun taking classes at a junior college in the fall of 1990. But I got my real education from my grandfather, whom I worked for at the same time. I went to school part-time, taking about two classes a semester, including through the winter and summer breaks. While juggling my course load, I learned the craft of the business from Abuelo. I slept at his house, rising at four thirty in the morning so I could accompany him to work. There, I witnessed firsthand how he achieved his success.

Years later, I would learn about "management by walking around," a technique famously coined by Hewlett-Packard cofounder David Packard in his book, *The HP Way*, which is exactly what it sounds like. My grandfather knew nothing about the HP way. He simply led his company in the way that felt right to him. That meant talking to everybody first thing on Mondays to ask how their weekends had been, how their family members were doing, and so forth. He would stop at every person's desk, sit down, and say, "Hello." And just by doing that, he held them accountable for the day. The door to his office, where he sat so that he faced out, was hardly ever closed.

At some point during the day, he would ask me to go to the ranch to check on the horses or deal with an issue on the property. Sometimes he sent me to the Rancho Santa Fe Polo Club, where, between my uncle and me, we stabled sixteen horses for us and another twenty for the pros. When I was done with the task at hand, I returned to the office to pick him up, go home together, and do the whole thing over again the next day. As part of my training, my grandfather wanted me to experience what it meant to juggle the customshouse brokerage, the ranch in Rosarito, and all the horses and hands in San Diego. I was back by my grandfather's side, just as I had been as a little kid on the ranch in Rosarito, and I loved every minute of it.

My uncle, however, was driving the Rosarito development project into the ground, not just with his handling of the finances but also through his decision-making. My dad had let Nando run with the project until the foundation of the shopping center was completed and construction on the frame was about to start. That's when Jefe discovered a huge problem with the architectural plans.

"Fernandito, you fucked this up, man!" my dad bellowed. "Where the fuck are your deliveries going to go? Where are the trucks going to deliver the goods to all the fucking stores, Fernando?"

Neither my uncle nor any of the people he had employed had seen fit to include a back alley behind the shopping center for deliveries and employee parking. This major screwup led my dad to wonder what else was going on with the project. It didn't take much investigating for him to discover that, the way things were going, they were going to run out of money before the development got completed. The banks weren't going to give Nando a pass like his indulgent parents always did.

"This isn't Monopoly money," Jefe seethed. "This is business, and we need to finish the job."

Nando waved him off. "Relax, it'll get done. Maybe we borrow a little more . . ."

My father erupted.

"You aren't doing shit! I'm the one dealing with the construction contracts and the men and their progress. And I'm telling you that we're almost dry. We can still finish if every cent that comes in on presales goes back into the project. Every cent."

Unlike most shopping centers that rent out their units, my father and uncle weren't looking to get into the business of running a mall. Instead, they were selling the units directly to retailers and would simply manage the property.

"You sound just like my father."

The insult wasn't lost on Jefe. If there was one thing my uncle couldn't tolerate, it was limits. Nando had a lot of unearned bravado, but even he didn't find it that easy to stand up to Jefe. There was my father's temper, sure. But even more important were his connections to the bank. My uncle, however, had a new source of confidence that pushed him past any fear he might have had of my father.

Nando had met Claudio Ruffo Appel while partying at Baby Rock, the Studio 54 of Mexico. The Tijuana mega-club with the rock-face

facade was the place to party in the '90s. The place was the very defini-
tion of over-the-top. Before the dancing kicked off around 11:00 p.m.,
there was usually some kind of performance that involved a light show
and professional dancers. Once, the dancers hid underneath the plants
inside the planters around the banquettes, rising up unexpectedly at
one point as part of the act. A person could climb a massive rock with
a waterfall and look down on the entire club. The Arellano Félix brothers of the Tijuana Cartel had a table there, as did Nando and I. In this
playground for the rich and ruthless, my uncle found a kindred spirit,
Claudio Ruffo Appel, whom everyone called Ruffo. He was the brother
of the governor of Baja California, Ernesto Appel.

Nando and Ruffo were instantly enamored with one another. They
played similar roles in their respective families, who saw each of them as
either rascal or scoundrel, depending on the day and whom you asked.
Their real bond, however, was partying. I'd thought Nando was a bon
vivant, but this guy was next level. The two men fueled each other like
a couple of addicts, encouraging one another's worst impulses.

Jefe despised Ruffo the minute he became close to my uncle. Our
hatred of the man was one thing my father and I agreed upon completely. Whenever I saw the sleazeball roll up to the ranch, I got a pit in
my stomach. It wasn't just that he walked in like he owned the place.
There was a menacing undercurrent in everything he said and did, like
the day he suggested my uncle take one of Abuelo's prized antique carriages "out for a spin to see what it can do." At the time, he and Nando
were super wasted on coke and booze. Neither man was introspective
even on his best day, but when they got fucked up, they didn't think at
all. To my horror, Nando got a nervous ranch hand to help him strap
two horses onto the carriage that had sat as a pristine ornament on the
road to the ranch for as long as I could remember.

"Picho!" shouted my uncle. Perched on the driver's seat, he patted
the spot next to his for me to join him.

I was just as drunk as my uncle that night, but there was no way I would have stepped foot in that carriage. I loved and respected my grandfather way too much. I shook my head. Nando shrugged as if I were the one who was lost. Then he turned his attention to the guests, who were hollering and chanting like Nando was a gladiator entering a coliseum. Egging the crowd on from the front and center was Ruffo, his weasel eyes ablaze as my uncle commanded the horses into a gallop that proved way too much for the one-hundred-plus-year-old carriage. Within minutes, my uncle crashed and destroyed the carriage. The terrified horses whinnied in the night while Nando sat on the ground laughing. I thought I was going to throw up.

Ruffo always took things too far. In Mexico, having a family member in politics was like having a green light to do whatever one wanted. In Ruffo's case, that was a lethal position to be in. When my dad and uncle stopped seeing eye to eye on the finances of the construction project, Ruffo took the opportunity to insinuate himself into Nando's business affairs. He stoked my uncle's sense of outrage and encouraged him to ditch his brother-in-law. Nando didn't need Jefe, argued Ruffo, who knew other people who could "help."

Ruffo wasn't Nando's only source of newfound confidence. My uncle also had finally married in 1992. Taking a page from my father's playbook, he'd chosen a woman from one of the oldest and richest families in the Tijuana–San Diego region.

Everything about Monique Estudillo made her the perfect match for Nando. She was adorable, the firecracker of her family. Although she was a cutie with a fun, raspy voice, Monique was also very smart and driven. A modern woman who'd been raised in macho TJ society, she could hold her own with men, no problem. Her spunk was also paired with a lot of grit. On her way to becoming an attorney, she'd earned law degrees both in Mexico and in the United States at the University of San Diego.

A lawyer to her core, she loved debating any subject, from politics to Mexico's best vocal artist. She was competitive and didn't mince words, not even when it came to Nando and other women. He was an irrepressible flirt, who showered attention on women—something he tried at first to do even when he was in Monique's presence. She wasn't having it, though.

"What are you doing? Who was that you were laughing with at the bar?" she might ask when Nando had taken too long to come back to our table at the restaurant.

"I'm just being nice," he would reply. Nando was always trying to use his charm to get out of trouble, but Monique didn't let him get away with it.

"Why are you being *nice*?"

"I'm a nice guy."

"You're making them think there's something there when you act 'nice,' so stop it."

Monique was a solid person from top to bottom, and so was her family. The Estudillos—considered one of a handful of "great families" of New Spain, the region of North and South America that was once part of the Spanish Empire—had helped to found TJ and San Diego. They were part of Old Town San Diego, California's first European settlement established in 1769, as evidenced by the Casa de Estudillo located in a historic state park. The family fled Old Town after the US invasion of 1846 and helped found Tijuana, where Monique's grandparents built a replica of the adobe Casa de Estudillo. They were no joke of a family. The patriarch, Monique's father, was a good businessman, upright and frugal.

My uncle conned all the Estudillos. Monique, who had no clue about my uncle's partying and profligate spending, fell head over heels for Nando. He sold her a bill of goods, convincing her he was an honest businessman who was developing his family's land in Rosarito. He showered her with lavish gifts and grand gestures, all of which cost money he didn't really have. And, of course, he cut a dashing figure on his horse in San Diego and at the ranch, a place that gave our families a common history. Back when Monique and her siblings were growing up, the Estudillos used to come to the ranch for riding lessons. So did the family of her aunt Carmen, whose husband, Rene Trevino, became the mayor of TJ. I was twenty around the time Monique and my uncle started dating, and I began dating Rene and Carmen's daughter, Monique's cousin Paola.

Monique and Nando had been together for less than a year when they decided to get married. This turn of events was a huge deal in our family. We figured that if anyone was going to be able to right the ship and control my uncle, it was going to be Monique: a tough chick with opinions, money, and a strong family.

That's why our family colluded in covering up all my uncle's flaws to shore up Nando's image as a prince. It was really hard to make my uncle smell good. Monique already took issue with his flirting. I can't imagine what she would have done if she'd found out he'd had girls over at the ranch the night before he threw a party there for her. Our efforts included keeping Ruffo, who had a shady rep in TJ, separate from Monique by never inviting them to the ranch at the same time. Despite the differences that existed between my grandparents and parents, we all were in cahoots in our efforts to keep Nando from screwing up the best thing to ever happen to him. We got him over the finish line, and he and Monique were wed at the ranch. I was his best man, and my grandfather broke his promise not to return to Mexico this one time, to see his son get married.

My father, however, was not at the wedding because he and Nando had locked horns over the land project a few months earlier. Egged on by Ruffo and emboldened by the Estudillo name, my uncle had decided he didn't need my father telling him what to do anymore. He wanted Jefe out of the deal. But to do that, he still needed one man: Abuelo.

"I want to move Pietro out," Nando told Abuelo. He blamed all the project's failings—like the fact that Nando needed to borrow more money—on Jefe. He was an asshole and impossible to work with, according to my uncle. That was music to Abuelo's ears. It almost didn't matter what else my uncle said: not even the fact that Nando wanted to use the rest of the property my grandfather owned as collateral. He said he needed it to finish the project, but in reality, he just wanted to continue his flamboyant lifestyle. It would be just until the sales on the housing development came through, my uncle said. After that, Nando promised, he'd pay everything back. My grandfather knew better than anyone that Nando was a terrible businessman and wholly unreliable. But his hate for my father was so great, he was willing to suspend disbelief and give his son his blessing.

My grandfather had put everything in my grandmother's name just in case anyone—from the government to some individual who might want to sue him—ever tried to come after him. This meant that Abuela had to sign bank documents for a second loan on the property—and she wasn't quite as happy as Abuelo was that her son-in-law was no longer part of the plan. She knew Nando and worried that the sums involved were big enough to cause a permanent rift between father and son.

Jefe was absolutely livid about getting screwed over by Nando— and he took his frustration out on my mom and me. Since he couldn't yell at the Gutierrez family, he yelled at the next best thing: us.

"Your fucking brother. God dammit," he said to my mother.

Or to me: "Who do you think got your grandfather out of jail! And this is how the big man thanks me?"

My mom and I just let him go off, wordlessly absorbing all the invectives directed at the relatives with whom we had the misfortune of sharing a bloodline. If we said one word in defense of my uncle, grandfather, or grandma, or if we even protested being subjected to

Jefe's abuse over their misdeeds, he only spiraled deeper and harder. He didn't stop his ranting for a long time.

It took months and months for him to stop obsessing over the fact that the Gutierrez family had rejected him, again.

~

About six months after my father was pushed out of the development project, Germán turned off Revolución and, two blocks off the main drag, pulled up to a small apartment house with a convenience store on the ground floor. Nando and Ruffo hopped out of the Range Rover, which looked out of place in this shady TJ neighborhood, and entered what Germán assumed was the building's basement through a metal door at the side of the store.

It wasn't until the men got back in the car that Germán knew why they had come to this part of town.

"Benjamin's actually a pretty likable guy," Nando said to Ruffo in the back seat.

They were talking about Benjamin Arellano, head of the infamous Tijuana Cartel or AFO, which at that time controlled the flow of drugs over the Tijuana–San Diego border and at one point supplied one-third of all cocaine that went into the US. Germán, aware of the rumors that Ruffo was close to the Arellanos, didn't know exactly what the meeting had been about, but he knew it hadn't been a social call. There were only a couple of reasons anyone got involved with *El Cártel de Tijuana*, and when it came to Nando, the most likely one was borrowing money.

By the summer of 1992, Nando had blown through the bank loans on polo and parties. Nothing my entire extended family did was ever light on expenses. We flew first class everywhere. My parents, grandparents, and uncle once spent $50,000 to rent four villas for a week-long vacation at Villa d'Este on the shores of Lake Como, where the entire family played like kings and queens. And now Monique, whom my uncle continued to shower with wealth he didn't really have, was expecting their first child.

Backed into a corner and most likely encouraged by Ruffo, Nando had taken a cash bailout from the Tijuana Cartel. It was the dumbest, most self-destructive move in the world. For all the greedy and risky things my dad had done in his life, even he knew never to borrow money from the Arellanos. During the '90s, Tijuana's streets were awash in blood spilled by the AFO, infamous for its "*baseballistas*" who used bats to beat to death people they'd hung from the rafters. The violence of *El Cártel de Tijuana* was legendary and gripping.

Germán was torn up inside about whether or not he should tell Don Fernando that his son had become somehow involved with the dangerous cartel. Germán never told secrets. Ever. But he knew that my uncle was on a very slippery slope and heading nowhere good. These were the most dangerous guys in all of Mexico. They hung people in the middle of the street with impunity. Germán would never have said anything unless he felt it was necessary to protect my uncle, and he would have done the same thing for me. We were his boys.

Finally, Germán steeled himself to tell my grandfather what he knew. It was July Fourth, 1992, a day filled with polo. Early in the day, my uncle and I played a big match—San Fernando against La Valencia, another prominent local family and polo rival—and won. That night, I was lucky enough to play in a big gala celebrity match at the Del Mar Polo Fields with Sylvester Stallone and William Devane. Abuelo was watching the indoor match from his private box. In his white pants, blue blazer, and Kangol hat, he looked every bit the king of the event. Everyone knew who Don Fernando was. Whether he was walking around the field offering greetings and champagne to everyone, including our opponents, or clicking his heels and kissing women's hands, he still possessed, at age seventy, the same class and charm that others had always found so engaging. My team won the celebrity match. It was my second trophy of the day, and my grandfather was beaming with pride. It had been a spectacular day. Abuelo looked at me and said, "You're just getting better and better."

After the evening match, Abuelo and I parted ways. I'd made a plan to go out with my friends for the Fourth. My grandfather was headed to the marina for an Independence Day party hosted by the Estudillos on their yacht. Notoriously tight with money, the Estudillo family had, thanks to their new son-in-law's influence, started to become bigger spenders. Nando had convinced Monique's father to buy a seventy-foot yacht, where the party was already underway.

Germán decided to use the drive from Del Mar to Coronado, when he was alone with his boss, to tell him about Nando and the Arellano cartel. Still, it took him almost fifteen to twenty miles into the thirty-mile drive to muster up the courage to spit it out.

"I have some news I do not want to tell you, but I have to tell you," Germán said, keeping his eyes on the road. "Your son is involved with the cartel through Ruffo. I believe he owes them money."

My grandfather, who had been completely in the dark about my uncle's involvement with the notorious criminal organization, was beyond shocked. Abuelo essentially controlled the San Ysidro border, but there were three things he never touched: people, guns, and drugs. Trafficking anything else, like alcohol or exotic animals, was fair game. He dealt with wealthy Mexicans and corrupt politicians. His realm was bribes, not *baseballistas*.

"*Muchas gracias*, Germán," Abuelo said, and then he went silent.

When he got mad, he went quiet—a trait I picked up from him. My grandfather was the opposite of my father, the Barker in Brioni. Because one could only imagine the fury behind his silence, it was much scarier.

I was passed out on my buddy Abel's couch after a fun night out with my boys when Abel woke me up. It was 1:30 a.m., and he had a worried expression on his face. "Pietro, we gotta get you out of here," he said nervously.

"What's going on?" I asked.

"I got to take you to your grandparents' house."

"Dude, you're scaring me."

But Abel wasn't answering my questions even as we got in his car, and I continued to ask him to tell me what was happening. Finally, he broke: "It's your grandfather."

The entire thirty-minute drive from Abel's house in Point Loma to Fairbanks, I was in shock. As we were closing in on Del Mar, an ambulance went by us, followed by Mom's car and my uncle's car.

I shouted at Abel, "Follow them!"

CHAPTER 14

DARK TIMES

Three days after we buried Abuelo, I was sitting at his desk in the customshouse office. The cherry wood stretched out before me, a sturdy reminder of the weighty responsibility I faced in running the business. *His* business.

I was still in shock that he was gone. As I had instructed, Abel had followed the ambulance to the hospital, where my grandfather was pronounced dead from a massive coronary. The news that Nando had borrowed money from the cartel had been too much for him to take. He had already been experiencing health problems. A few months before his heart attack, his employees expressed concern to him when he arrived in the office one morning with one side of his face slumped lower than the other.

"*Me dio un escalofrío,*" he had replied, attributing one side of his face going numb to "a chill," instead of the more scientific cause of a stroke. A stereotypical macho Mexican man, he had convinced everyone he was fine.

But Abuelo had also been trying to take care of his health. He was seeing a cardiologist, who'd had Abuelo cut way back on his drinking, take walks in the mornings and afternoons, and lose a little weight. I can only imagine how much he drank at the Estudillos' July Fourth party to medicate himself after his brief conversation with Germán. Either the stress of his disappointing son's latest blunder or the booze, or both, had been too much for his heart.

His death came as a shock to everybody. He'd been a bull of a man who up until his dying day woke up at five in the morning to be the first one in the office. As I've said, his harrowing time in jail had weakened him. But even after that experience, he'd been more robust than most men and over the years had remained our family's pillar of strength. When I arrived at the customs agency the day after his funeral, his employees' faces were more incredulous than sad. Some shook their heads in disbelief. I knew exactly how they felt. The difference was, they were all looking at me to answer the question: What happens now?

That's when, sitting at Abuelo's massive desk, it hit me: "Fuck. This is real. I have three hundred employees. I'm responsible for three hundred families."

In the last few years of his life, my grandfather had finally accepted that his son was never going to take over the family business, and he had shifted his attention from Nando to me. He had taught me the accounting functionalities of the agency: not just how much money it brought in but also what he spent on the business and why. I had the experience I needed to manage the whole operation. I only had to take the reins. I had just turned twenty-two.

My uncle didn't argue about my taking over the family import-export business. Not even his father's death could persuade him to take an interest. We both knew he wouldn't be any good at it anyway. Plus, he still needed to deal with the Plaza San Fernando development.

I told him, "You need to focus on the property and fix this shit." I didn't know how deep his financial problems went, though.

After my grandfather died, my dad was at first the only one in the family who knew about Nando's involvement with the Tijuana

Cartel—and that's only because the cartel came to him. By that point, Nando had already begun to miss payments on the loan, which was not something a person did with the Arellano brothers. "You've got to jump in," a rep from the cartel told Jefe, "because that young man right there is going to fuck it all up and end up dead."

The cartel delivered the same message to Nando, who knew he had no choice but to bring my dad back into the development deal.

Shortly after my uncle asked Jefe to return to the project, my dad had a frank conversation with Abuela, since now, with Don Fernando gone, she had ultimate control over the property. Their relationship had always been better than the one between my father and grandfather. Still, Jefe wanted to make sure she knew just how crucial he was to the success of everyone's future. He told her in no uncertain terms that Nando had made a deal with the wrong people and only he could help him now. Without her husband to fall back on, my grandmother was forced to confront her son's inadequacies. She was terrified of losing her golden boy to the Arellanos. She had no other option but to give my father her full support.

She believed that my father could turn Plaza San Fernando around. He had, after all, made good on his promise to get Don Fernando out of jail. However, she would never openly express her confidence in my dad. That way, if the development deal went south, she could make sure her son-in-law took the heat for its failure and keep Nando's life out of danger.

I was surprised and scared when I found out Tio Fer was in bed with the Arellano cartel. I had been busy running the customshouse brokerage firm, which was responsible at that time for putting food on the table for the entire family. After Abuelo died, however, all the hidden agendas came out in the open. There was no room for secrets once everything became about survival. The only thing I didn't know was how big my uncle's debts were. Whether because he was embarrassed or because he was trying to protect me, Nando never spoke to me directly about the situation with the cartel. Instead, we started to spend less time with each other. He hardly came to the brokerage office anymore, and that's where I spent my days.

Jefe jumped back into the Rosarito land project, which had the potential to become a very valuable piece of property. He wasn't worried about getting on the cartel's bad side, because he was confident he could fix the mess Nando had made. My father was a fixer. That's what he did. Once he had power of attorney over every single one of my grandmother's properties, he set to work. But it was going to take a lot of time and energy to save the project, and both of those were in short supply, as my dad's other business ventures were also floundering.

He was becoming increasingly desperate in his pursuit of the sports book license. He had been sinking most of our assets into the deal, so that by 1993 he had not only spent all the money he earned during his years in the exchange, he'd also put two mortgages on our house in Coronado. He had also browbeat his partners to work their so-called foolproof connections harder, in order to move the process along. But even with all that, they still didn't have enough money to satisfy the men who pulled the strings.

Then one day, as his resources dwindled and his temper flared, he stupidly decided to bite the hand that fed him. As the bagman for Garza's tax scams, he thought he could extort more money out of the deal. It was a huge risk to attempt such a thing, but the wins in front of him—in the form of controlling the racetrack's betting—were too big for him not to take that risk.

The next time he collected the money from Garza's latest victim, Jefe didn't hand over Garza's portion per their usual routine. "If you want some of this money, I need a bigger cut," my dad threatened.

Garza was no one to be trifled with, and my dad was trifling with him big-time.

"Go fuck yourself," Garza said. He shut Jefe down immediately, but my dad didn't get the message. Instead, more pissed off than ever, he escalated the fight. Garza had told him no, but my father followed through on his threat. Whether out of desperation or ego, he hung on to Garza's money, and his relationship with one of the most feared men in Mexico went sideways, to put it mildly.

The two men went to war. Their fight was very ugly and very public, and neither of them came out ahead. It was a classic Mexican stand-off. My dad used the only weapon he had against Garza—the media.

He attacked Garza in the papers, and Garza's political reputation was destroyed. My dad knew firsthand about all the tax scams Garza had run and was willing to provide all the gory details to journalists, who were more than happy to run scandalous stories about the high-up government minister. Jefe made a few reporters' careers, even though it meant exposing himself in the process.

It was yet another case of my father's temper getting in the way of his judgment. Jefe simply didn't care what it meant to tarnish the name of a man who everyone else was too scared to challenge. Never mind the fact that the Mexican government *just happened* to put a big tax lien on the customshouse building after my father launched his media attack, or the fact that Garza cut my father off completely from the scams that had been his primary source of income. It wasn't the first time my dad had taken the scorched-earth approach, and it wouldn't be the last.

Jefe now found himself with zero income coming in while all his cash was tied up in the sports book deal. When the mortgage payment on the house came due, he didn't have $12,000 in the bank to cover it. I didn't know any of this. All I knew was that one day he told me to give him my Rolex.

"Dad, Nando gave me this watch."

"I fucking need it."

So I handed over the gold Rolex with a diamond face and emerald numbers. This wasn't because I knew how close he was to foreclosure on our home or that pawning the watch would buy him a couple of months of mortgage payments. I didn't know any of that. I was only thinking about my mom. If Jefe said he needed something and didn't get it, my mom would be the one to pay. I didn't want him going after her, hounding her until she was forced to beg me to give him what he wanted. No watch, no matter how expensive or sentimental, was worth sacrificing Ama's peace of mind to one of Jefe's rampages.

"You shouldn't have to go through this," Ama said when he took the watch. "This is not what I meant for your life."

"I still have the Rolex you guys gave me," I said, referencing the Rolex Submariner they had bought for me when I was eight years old. "The other one was just a flashy watch to show that we have money. This is the one that's important to me."

She knew I was trying to make her feel better, just as I knew what she was trying to do by acknowledging my experience. Now we were the ones dancing around disappointment.

Our feelings were not on my father's radar. He didn't give a shit that my mother and I were sad when Jefe and Garza had their falling-out. He probably didn't think about our feelings at all. The Garza family had been our close friends, and we were going to miss them. The vacations, plastic surgery recuperations, fast cars: we'd had so many memorable times together. We even once played a prank together.

In 1992, the Garzas were in town to evaluate a few of their properties in Tijuana they planned to remodel and had brought an architect from Mexico City to evaluate the scope of the projects. When the Garzas told the architect they were going to have dinner that evening at La Strada with their good friend Pietro La Greca, a look of surprise came across his face.

"The godfather?" he asked. The architect had apparently heard of my dad. Like a game of telephone, Jefe's reputation had become distorted as it traveled, so that by the time the architect heard of him, he had grown into a powerful and bloodthirsty mafioso.

Amused by this impression, the Garzas did not disabuse the architect of it. Instead, they told us about it. We were equally tickled and together devised a plan to really fuck with this architect.

After touring the properties, the Garzas told the architect they were going to "visit a friend in Coronado." Our home on the water was the site of an elaborate ruse. At six foot four and 250 pounds, I was a big dude who hung out with a lot of guys, football and basketball players, who were just as big. I enlisted a few of them to play bodyguards for "the godfather." Having bought fake machine guns from a costume shop, I installed a couple of my friends on the balconies of the house. It was funny to see one of my buddies, a three-hundred-pound lineman, pacing back and forth.

My pal Jim and I, also pretending to be security guards, let the Garzas into the house, but we stopped the architect and roughly patted him down before letting him pass. He appeared nervous while I frisked him, but I thought he was actually going to pass out when he saw my father in a white suit, white shirt, white shoes, red tie, and dark Porsche Carrera gold-framed aviators that were a little too big. In a scene straight out of *Scarface*, my father stood for a moment at the top of the circular staircase that led down to the foyer. Then he descended, walking right past the architect, whom I held by the back of his shirt. My dad didn't even acknowledge the presence of the architect, who I could now feel physically shaking. Then, with a theatrical flourish, my father turned around and waved the architect in. But the architect didn't move. He was paralyzed with fear.

Even those who had been in on the prank broke out in laughter. But suddenly, I didn't find it so funny. The poor man was so scared, he was shaking. Even after we told him it was all a joke, that the guns were fake and that Jefe wasn't a godfather, the guy still didn't stop shaking. Instead, he ran to the bathroom. In fact, he was traumatized for the rest of the afternoon and evening. At dinner that night at La Strada, I noticed he didn't take a sip of his wine or touch his pasta. Meanwhile, my dad, Garza, and the rest of the group were still laughing about it, which made my stomach churn.

I wasn't just bothered by the fact that everyone else seemed too self-centered or insensitive to take notice of the architect's state. The man also seemed to know something that I didn't. What is the saying about there being a grain of truth in every joke? My dad seemed a little too good at his role to be simply playacting. Perhaps my father had a little mafioso in him after all. It certainly seemed that way. Because when the sports book deal eventually fell through, Jefe responded like he was a real-life member of Cosa Nostra.

Whenever he wanted something, whether it was opening up his first foreign exchange or winning the bid to run the racetrack, he was all in. But he was especially possessed when it came to going after the sports book, an operation so lucrative, it made his foreign-exchange empire look like chump change. Unfortunately, he was trying to move too aggressively, and he was pissing off the other partners in the group by rushing the negotiations.

In addition, Jefe tended to erupt like a volcano, and that was complicating his business relationships. His was a desperate anger. He had leveraged everything we owned, including our home, to come up with the money he needed for the bid. Now, the tension was getting to him. He was unable to control his behavior.

Over time, his impatience turned into bald aggression that cost him his relationship with his and his friend Hector's two partners, and finally with Hector himself. The other men were the first to want to get rid of my father, but Hector repeatedly convinced them to give him another chance. That is, until he couldn't take it anymore either. Once they all were fed up with El Italiano, the group gave him the boot, not long before winning the concession. They had already pushed him out by the time they signed the deal.

My dad's wrath was biblical, and he reserved the bulk of his rage for Hector, whom he blamed for not protecting his interests with the rest of the bidding group. He was so angry, he hired someone to beat up Hector. This was some real godfather shit. The henchman didn't just scare Hector; he beat him to a pulp. Hector wound up in the hospital.

He almost died, but he didn't. Instead, he sued us. In 1994, Hector filed a civil suit for $20 million against my dad in a US court. My dad couldn't defend himself because there was plenty of evidence against him: pictures of Hector's injuries, the physician's reports, and reports of my father telling anyone who would listen how he'd had Hector beat up. Once again, my father had been willing to fuck himself over just to keep himself from looking like a fool. At least, *he* didn't think he looked like a fool.

It was a pretty foolish move, especially since Jefe didn't have the money to defend himself. The best my father could afford was a crack-pot attorney, and he could retain that guy for only two or three months. He had no other alternative than to declare bankruptcy. In the end, Hector got nothing, because my father had nothing.

Or, more accurately, *we* had nothing. Once my dad began filing for bankruptcy during the lawsuit, my dad started to sell off everything our family owned.

The rift with Garza, on top of the rift that cost him the sports book, crushed our family. We had to sell the house in Coronado and everything in it, which included all the furniture my dad had bought in Italy. It had taken three shipping containers sent from Italy to San Diego to outfit our ten-thousand-square-foot home. From the Lladró figurines to the custom Murano chandeliers that graced every room in the house, it all had to go. In the end, the house—and forty-foot yacht we kept in front—was already so badly leveraged that the profit from the sale was less than $300,000 on a $3 million home.

Those were dark times. Jefe sold all the watches, the jewelry, the cars. He sold all of Ama's jewelry, too, including the sixty-five-carat diamond he'd bought for a quarter of a million dollars in Vegas. The sale of her "ugly diamond" wasn't the one that got to her, however. Although it killed her to sell the stuff we owned, she was mostly stoic about our family financially crumbling. She held her shit together—never crying or yelling—despite her fears over how we were going to survive. But a look of disappointment and sadness did peek through when my dad took a set of rubies that had been a gift from my grandfather, along with the engagement ring my father had bought her to replace the smaller diamond ring he gave her when they were first married. Seeing how that hurt her, my dad said, "I've got to do it, but I'll get them back for you."

The sale of our belongings was a crushing experience for all of us. Jefe was too embarrassed to pawn the stuff in San Diego, so he drove up to Newport Beach, where there was a high-end pawnshop. Once he showed me where the place was, he made me do the fucking eighty-five-mile drive to Newport Beach's Balboa Island from downtown San Diego, where the three of us had moved into a condo. It sucked having to be the one to sell my mom's beautiful jewelry because my dad didn't have the balls to. I should have been much more pissed off than I was. At the time, I was too busy worrying about my mom to process how mad I was at my father for screwing over our family.

Having two projects collapse in quick succession, in part because of personal belligerence, might cause some men to reflect. But not my dad. He simply diverted all his aggression toward the only financial resource he had left: the Rosarito land project. Just as he had goaded Garza and the sports book men, he began pushing my uncle to speed up the development.

There was an important difference between my uncle and those other men, however. Unlike them, Nando was more than happy to let my father do the day-to-day grind work of turning around the San Fernando Plaza.

From that point on, Jefe threw himself into every aspect of the project, driving out to Rosarito every day—even on weekends—to check firsthand on the progress of the construction workers and to shore up the finances. My dad also turned his attention to my grandmother, making sure to meet with her often to keep her apprised of how the development and loan payments were moving along. He put her at ease, assuring her that everything was headed in the right direction. The cartel was getting its payments, which meant that her son was safe.

My dad wasn't just putting one over on her. The shopping center site was back up and running. Sales were again coming in for the stores that were under construction. Units that had already been sold to retailers, who'd threatened to sue because of all the delays, were now finally being finished.

Nando, however, didn't care for the way my father ran the finances. Once he was back in charge, Jefe kept a tight grip on the purse strings so that Nando couldn't squander any more money. Maybe that's why my uncle went ahead and made the dumbest of all his moves in what had been a long career of dumb moves.

A year after my dad had come back into the project, Nando booted him out again.

There was no reason to do such a thing unless he had a death wish. For some reason, though, my uncle wasn't scared of the consequences. The cartel had insisted on my father's involvement, and they didn't like it when anyone defied orders. But Nando was still hanging out with Ruffo, who brought out the worst side of my uncle.

When the reins had been handed back to him a year earlier, Jefe had made it clear that Ruffo was in no way, shape, or form allowed to get near the development. Ruffo, who had insinuated himself into the project inasmuch as it served his greed, didn't like the new arrangement, and he worked on my uncle until Nando came around to his way of thinking and talked Abuela into getting rid of my dad.

Everyone knew that my uncle was self-destructive, but what was my grandmother's excuse when she let him talk her into revoking my father's power of attorney a second time? Maybe she was just foolish to believe the garbage he fed her about the project being far enough along that he could handle the rest to the cartel's satisfaction. More likely, she wasn't able to say no to her golden boy. She never could refuse him anything.

Whatever her reasoning, the result was the same: my dad was cut out. It was the ultimate slap in the face. At risk to himself and our family, he had saved my uncle's life and my grandmother's fortune. And this was the thanks he got? Thrown out like yesterday's trash.

He screamed a little bit about my uncle running back to his mommy, crying to get what he wanted. But then my father went quiet, and he never went quiet. It was eerie. He was done and said as much when he told my mother: "I'm no longer able to protect your brother."

CHAPTER 15

Silk Diapers and Snakes

Jefe had been expecting a call from the cartel.

"What's going on?" one of the men asked him over the phone. "We haven't gotten a payment in the last two months. The plaza looks like it's stalled. What the fuck is happening?"

When Nando and Abuela revoked his power of attorney on Plaza San Fernando, my dad did not inform the Tijuana Cartel. He decided to wait until Nando fucked up and the cartel came to him. It was a calculated move. If he had called the cartel to inform them that he had been kicked out of the project, they would have told him to get back in. Then he would have been in an impossible situation of negotiating between two irrational sides.

Having anticipated correctly that Nando would neither reach out to the cartel to tell them about the new arrangement nor follow through on making the payments, Jefe played dumb when he got the call.

"Nando didn't tell you what happened? I assumed he'd call you," Jefe told the Arellano heavy, lying through his teeth. "I'm not involved anymore," he continued. "He got rid of me again."

"What? Well, let's get you back in."

"I'm sorry. Fernando is out of my control."

My dad had completely washed his hands of Nando and the Gutierrez family. After spending years secretly hoping for their approval—first by having a son, then by getting Don Fernando out of jail, and finally by saving Nando's ass from the TJ Cartel, at least for a while—he had finally given up.

Jefe's friction with my mother's family had never been an easy thing for her. From the moment she broke the news to her conservative family that she was pregnant out of wedlock to El Italiano, Ama had had to negotiate between her husband and the rest of her family. When Abuelo and Nando kicked my father out of the land development deal the first time, my mom, unsure who was being honest, had found herself caught in the middle of the warring camps. Although Jefe didn't want her to talk to them during that time, she'd maintained a cordial if not distant relationship.

The second time around, however, was too much even for my mom. Her mother's decision totally defied logic. Why would she mess up the project just when everything was going right? There was only one reason. Her mother could never deny her little brother anything, even something that would destroy their family. This wasn't just an issue of the money and land. This was life-and-death. My mom stopped talking to her mother and brother.

Though my dad could be a mean son of a bitch, Ama knew that, in this case, he was protecting her interests. Back when he still had power of attorney, he had worked to liberate several of Abuelo's properties from the cartel by paying back the loans Nando had taken out on them with the Félix brothers. Little by little, Jefe had secretly held back just enough of the money earmarked for the development to pay back the cartel and clear the loan they held on a few of Abuelo's properties. This included the customshouse building and a complex of warehouses in Tijuana. The really tricky maneuver my dad pulled was to put official liens in my mother's name on those properties he'd free from the cartel's grip. It was a legal maneuver, based on the fact that my mother had a right to a portion of the proceeds of her father's inheritance. But practically speaking, it meant that if my uncle tried to take out another loan on them in any way, he couldn't. It was a brilliantly weird move by my dad, and the kind of devious play only he could conceive. The properties were still in Abuela's name, but as far as Jefe was concerned, they belonged to my mother, and he planned on making sure she inherited her birthright.

Unlike my mother and father, I still had a relationship with my uncle, mostly because I was running the import-export business. As Abuelo's son, Nando had officially inherited the customs license. But I continued to manage the entire operation. My uncle didn't even come into the office anymore. Since I was doing the work, my dad thought I should at least own half the business—even if my grandfather had never promised me anything like that.

Jefe was on my ass, asking every week, "Have you gotten your fifty percent?" I had tried four or five times, and each time I was met with the *mañana* syndrome.

"Absolutely!" my uncle said as he raced out the door after picking up the last of his personal effects from the office. "You deserve it!" In follow-up phone calls, he always said the same thing: "That hasn't been done yet?" It was the classic runaround. Nando was holding on tight to his inheritance.

"You have to stay in that office until you do," my dad warned.

That's exactly where I was—sitting in my grandfather's chair in the office at San Ysidro—the day in January of 1996 when Carlos, one of the managers at the brokerage firm, stuck his head in. I was just finishing up a meeting with the two ladies who handled all the brokerage's accounting, and I could see the look of fear on Carlos's face.

"Pichito, there are two officers here who want to see you," he said.

I told Carlos to bring them in. My heart dropped into my stomach when the two men in suits showed me their badges. FBI. My mind flashed on a memory from when we were on the lam, after the FBI had warned us to get out of Beverly Hills. My father had explained to me then that the FBI has an obligation to warn an American citizen if they get intel that tells them that person's life is in danger.

"Are you Fernando Gutierrez Jr.?" one of them asked.

"No. Is this urgent?"

"Yes, it is a matter of life or death."

Life or death.

"Let me get him on the phone right now," I said.

I had spent enough time with my security guard Alex and other ex-military types hired by my dad to know that, for my own protection, I needed to be completely transparent while in the presence of the two agents. I have a healthy fear of American law enforcement. If I was ever stopped in my car by a cop, I rolled the window down all the way and made sure my hands were on the steering wheel at my ten and two.

In this moment, I did not want them to think that I was trying to tip my uncle off. I put the phone on speaker and dialed Nando's number. He picked up.

"Unc, I'm here at the office," I said. "I have two FBI officers with me, and they need to speak with you."

"Walk them to the waiting room by my office, and I'll be there as soon as I can," he said, following quickly with, "Pichito, *que quieren?*"

I knew not to speak a word of Spanish.

"I don't know what they want," I said, carefully translating my uncle's question into my answer.

No more than ten minutes later, Nando walked into the agency. He headed straight back to his office without saying a word. He gave me a quick look as he passed, raising his eyebrows, not in alarm but with the kind of smirk a class clown might wear while being called into the principal's office.

I was so pissed off. Nando didn't give a fuck about anyone. He was smirking? This wasn't a goddamn joke. He didn't take anything seriously—not his father's business, not even his own life. I decided he didn't care about me either. The cartel was clearly after my uncle, and my proximity to him put a target on my back too.

I knew what I had to do. I grabbed my car keys and nothing else, nodded goodbye to Carlos and the ladies in accounting, and left. For good. It was a painful decision to walk away from an eighty-year-old family business with more than three hundred employees that generated more than $250,000 per month. However, I didn't hesitate for one second in making that decision. No amount of money was worth catching a stray bullet.

My father agreed. As much as he had hounded me to stake my claim over the agency before, as soon as the FBI agents paid their visit, he was equally firm in saying: "You're not going back."

My dad wanted me to watch my back, but he wasn't panicked. None of us talked to Nando in the days after the FBI visit, though we understood that the agents had undoubtedly warned him that his life was at risk. And we assumed that he wouldn't change his ways, even after getting their warning. He never did.

Jefe continued to operate as if it were business as usual until three or four months after the FBI showed up at the brokerage house, following the terrifying murder of his longtime employees and close associates Angelo and Alfredo. The newspapers subsequently reported that the men had been killed during a robbery. In fact, Alfredo and Angelo had been taking $30,000 to deposit in the bank when they left the foreign exchange in TJ. But whoever shot them left the money behind.

That was no robbery. It was a hit.

At the time of his death, Angelo knew all my dad's secrets, which meant he knew the secrets of the richest, most powerful, and corrupt people in Mexico. Throughout his career, Angelo had functioned for Jefe much the way my dad had for Garza. He'd done my father's bidding, or, rather, his dirty work. Angelo was the one who'd dropped off or picked up the briefcases of cash that oiled the money-laundering operation back when it was still in business. Not my dad.

"I just don't know who did this," my dad said when he told my mom and me the news. A man as proud as my father would never say that he was scared, but the look of fear in his eyes was unmistakable.

Ama started crying. She and Angelo had known each other since they were sixteen. Over the years, as he had become the keeper of more and more of my dad's secrets, his relationship with her had grown more distant. I always noticed that whenever Angelo came around the house, he greeted my mother as if he were ashamed of something, his head hanging down as he gave her a quick "*Cómo estás*, Maria?" He always avoided eye contact, and he seemed like he couldn't get out of our house fast enough. He had once been her friend. But since the day my mom found out he had hidden that my father was dating four other girls while courting her, she hadn't trusted Angelo in the same way.

Now, at last, Angelo had become a casualty of my father's secrets. He knew too many of them—the mechanics of how and where illegal money flowed—and someone needed those secrets to be kept, no matter the cost. The obvious culprit was the TJ Cartel, but my father had other ideas. He believed Garza was behind the murder of his longtime trusted employees. And Garza was much stealthier than the brutal but obvious Arellano brothers. There would be no warnings when Garza came for you.

"Do we have anything to worry about?" Ama asked.

"I don't know," he said, biting his pinkie finger deeply into the corner of the right side of his mouth and shaking his head. That was his tell that he was, indeed, very worried.

From that point on, my parents were no longer simply laying low. They went into full lockdown. This was especially difficult for my father. My dad was a guy who liked to be out and about, whether that was holding court at La Strada or making up some excuse for a trip to Home Depot. Home was a cage for him. He didn't like TV, and he didn't drink. Holed up in the small townhouse they had in a gated community in Rancho Santa Fe after moving from San Diego, he sat in front of his computer, surfing the early internet. I would constantly be cleaning up viruses because he clicked on everything from Italian news sites to phony sweepstakes to free porn.

He wanted me to stay with them, but in 1995, I was in my last semester at USD, earning an undergraduate degree in business, and I didn't want to quit the only thing I had left. I had continued to attend junior college for two years while working for Abuelo. By 1993, I had been able to transfer to USD with enough credits to complete my degree in less than two years. Using the same part-time schedule I employed in junior college, taking a lighter course load throughout the entire year including summer and winter breaks, I would go on to earn my college degree, something that I am still proud of. It's hard to concentrate on a paper about procurement when the FBI has just told you there's a target on your back.

I was still in school, though, at the time, and that semester, I had rented an apartment in downtown San Diego for $890 a month. I definitely didn't want to move back in with my dad, who was now a caged animal. Instead, we agreed that I would only leave my apartment to go to class. I had to call him when I got to class and when I got home.

It was only a matter of time before tragedy hit. It felt like we were just waiting for something bad to happen. This explains why Mom's tone was so calm when she called me on December 11, 1996.

"Turn on channel eight news," she said.

There was the standard line, warning viewers of graphic images, and then a white sheet draped over a body. In camera footage taken on the scene, I saw my uncle's dark curls, matted in blood, peeking out over the top of the sheet. My mom and I were both quiet on the phone. When the news had moved on to a different story, I said, "They got him." My uncle was thirty-eight years old.

As the *L.A. Times* reported, the Tijuana Cartel was famous for its public displays of shocking violence, but this "bold, gangland-style murder" was newsworthy because it happened in a wealthy section of

San Diego. The scene of that killing, the article read, was not Tijuana but California, a picturesque beach strip known as the Silver Strand in the seaside community of Coronado, one of San Diego's most exclusive zip codes. The Arellano Félix brothers respected the United States border. It was practically a rule that they kept their business in Mexico. However, they made an exception to execute my uncle.

> Fernando Jesus Gutierrez Jr. was driving his white Mercedes-Benz coupe to his elegant suburban residence at dinnertime Wednesday when an expert marksman—or marksmen—pulled alongside and pumped five shots into his face, escaping into rush-hour traffic, authorities say.

After he was hit, Nando's car skidded two hundred yards before jumping the highway and landing in the San Diego Bay's surf line, just in time for rush hour. The freeway was shut down until 9:00 a.m. the next morning, creating a massive morning rush-hour traffic jam. Nando went out like he lived: as an over-the-top pain in the ass.

The state judicial police in Tijuana had outstanding arrest warrants for my uncle that stemmed from his defrauding the bank on the land loans. The *L.A. Times* quoted a member of this police force as saying, "If you treat people badly, they end up hating you."

The law enforcement official further told the newspaper that Nando had come from a very well-respected Mexican family, but he wound up nothing like his old man. "His son turned out to be a little devil," the official said, referencing my grandfather and uncle, "born into opulence, with silk diapers."

Nando's funeral was fit for a prince. It was held at The Immaculata, the majestic cathedral on the campus of USD with twenty side chapels and a seating capacity of nine hundred. It took a venue as large as that sprawling Catholic church to accommodate all the people who turned out to mourn my uncle. The man had loved to party and would be missed by many.

My father was persona non grata at the funeral. Monique, my grandmother . . . nobody from that side of the family wanted him there. They felt he could have done more to protect Nando against the cartel.

Our family debated whether my mom and I should attend. Out of an abundance of caution, Jefe didn't think I should go, and I agreed with him. Until my dad was able to make sure everything was settled with the cartel, he wanted me to stay out of view.

Ama was a different story. Her problem with going to the funeral didn't involve the cartel, though, or the FBI. Her problem was her family. Monique and Abuela blamed everything that had happened on my dad. In their eyes, Jefe was a villain and Nando, a saint. Maybe Monique was protecting the image of her dead husband for their son, Fernando Gutierrez III. I had never met Nando's son, because he was born after I broke ties with my uncle on the heels of the FBI's arrival at the customshouse.

Until the day he died, Nando had stuck to his lie that the Rosarito land project was in jeopardy because my father stole all the money. But the real crime, in my grandmother's and Monique's eyes, was Nando's death. They both believed that by not intervening further, my father had signed a warrant for my uncle's death. They weren't completely wrong.

The fact was, Jefe hadn't stolen from either Nando or the Gutierrez family. He hadn't stolen from the Arellano cartel either. In fact, Dad had tried to save my uncle from himself—all while earning his own profit, of course. Jefe had made sure that construction was moving ahead and that the cartel was receiving regular payments—until Nando got rid of him. For my father, that was the last straw. He stopped doing anything to protect my uncle. So did he kill him? I guess that's a matter of interpretation.

I knew both men as well as anybody could, and I feel confident in saying there were no heroes in this story. Despite the narrative that my uncle had cultivated, and that the Gutierrez side chose to believe, my father wasn't solely to blame. And yet he wasn't blameless. My uncle and dad shared a certain creative bent to the truth. Both knew how to sprinkle just enough facts into a story to create doubt, even if what they were saying wasn't right.

My mom knew this about her husband and brother. She also wasn't going to disavow Jefe just to appease her mother, whom she still blamed for letting Nando get away with, if not murder, then bank fraud. Plus, Ama needed my dad more than ever, now that the Gutierrez clan had completely crumbled and all the land Don Fernando had spent a lifetime acquiring was in jeopardy.

Although my mom wasn't exactly welcome at the funeral, she loved her brother and wanted to say goodbye. So with the support of her three best friends, she went to the service. There, she exchanged a cordial kiss with her mother, but she was not invited to sit up front with my grandmother and Monique.

While my mom was at the funeral, I thought about the last time I'd seen my uncle, a memory I have returned to countless times. The encounter happened not long after I left the customs agency, at a Gipsy Kings concert in San Diego. Tio Fer and I hadn't been in touch for months, because of the family divide. But when we found each other sitting in the same row at the concert, we instantly walked toward one another and embraced. Everyone else in our groups scooted down so we could sit next to each other, and for a few hours, we sat side by side, listening to the music. We didn't exchange words until the concert ended. Then Nando turned to me and asked, "Do you want to go out?"

"Unc, you know we can't."

"I know," he said, giving me a sad smile.

We hugged again and said goodbye.

Deep down, I believed my uncle wasn't a bad guy. He was spoiled and willful and impulsive. But we all covered up a lot of shit for him, because he was also fun, openhearted, generous, and loving. He was also swimming in waters that were too deep for him. We all deceived ourselves when it came to Nando. Perhaps Nando deceived himself most of all. Ultimately, that deception led to his demise, and to the demise of our family.

Nando's death was the catalyst for the end of everything. My grandmother and Monique blamed my father, but Nando was the one who had taken things too far with a famously dangerous cartel. My mom was caught in the middle, but ultimately she had to side with my father, who had her best interests in mind and, even more importantly to her, mine.

In the end, we lost, to the banks and the cartel, most of the empire my grandfather had spent his life working to build. The ranch, the Plaza San Fernando project, and all that land from the ocean to the mountains that my grandfather had squatted was gone. So were two buildings on a main road in TJ.

The bank also foreclosed on my grandparents' beautiful Fairbanks house in Rancho Santa Fe. To have the last home Abuelo had lived in taken away from my grandfather was painful enough. But in a twist out of some bad novel, it was bought at auction by none other than Rocky De La Fuente, my dad's old foreign-exchange competitor. My mom was hurt. I was outraged. Our old "family friend" had purchased the house in which my grandfather died.

I didn't want anything to do with Rocky after that. But my dad saw an opportunity. He decided to appeal to Rocky's sense of guilt and get Rocky to rent his old house in La Jolla to my father for a good deal. And that's exactly what he did.

I got it: Jefe was a survivor. He'd needed to find a decent place for my mom to live. That was one thing. But going over to Rocky's for the holidays, at my grandparents' old home? That was entirely out of the question. I told him there was no way I was going over there for Christmas dinner.

"You're coming!" my father yelled.

"No, I'm not!" I yelled back. "What a lowlife piece of fucking shit, buying that house!"

Christmas wasn't just Christmas to me; December 25 was also my grandfather's birthday. So the holidays had always been a magical time for our family. They started on December 23 when Abuelo and I sat under the tree, setting up the beautiful train set he received as a gift one year from my mom and grandmother. He had turned the process of assembling the train into an annual tradition. More accurately, he'd mostly watch me put it together and then fix whatever was needed. Even as a young boy, I could tell how much pleasure the tradition brought him.

He was the kind of guy who cherished special moments and took note of them. Every time we saw a sunset from the ranch, he would stand up, raise one hand, and say, "Thank you for another beautiful day, Mr. Sun." While I attached the locomotive to the train cars under the Christmas tree, Abuelo reached out and touched my hair. The moment was not about gifts or money. It wasn't about anything but being together. He really loved me.

My mom and uncle had had their own holiday tradition of exchanging gag gifts. These weren't ugly sweaters or coffee mugs with lewd sayings that they traded. No, Ama and Nando played out their rivalry-tinged love through absurd gifts. The best were the crazy ones that neither of them could return or throw away.

One Christmas, my uncle, the ultimate prankster, gifted my mother a miniature horse. "What am I supposed to do with a miniature horse?" she cried in delight. Bianca wound up living at the house in Coronado for a while until my dad said it was time for her to move on to the ranch. My uncle had a tiny carriage constructed and took a photo of my mom sitting in it behind Bianca in her harness. Ama and Nando had gotten a kick out of that gift, and out of each other.

Now, I could only look back on the time when we'd all gathered around the big Christmas dinner table—laden with the most sumptuous dishes, including Teresita's *buñuelos*—everyone engaged in lively debates fueled by flowing champagne. I wished it could have just stayed like that. But it hadn't. Nothing stayed the same. I knew that.

My father always won every argument he had. This included our argument about going to Abuelo's former home to celebrate Christmas at Rocky's table. He explained why he had to accept the invitation. He told me he understood better than anyone how a vindictive, egocentric guy like Rocky operated because he was just like him.

"You have to understand," my dad said, "snakes don't bite snakes."

CHAPTER 16

REUNION

In August 1997, I waited for my parents in an airy suite on the twenty-fifth floor of Waikiki Beach's Ala Moana Hotel. We had been apart for seven months. This was by far the longest span of time I had ever spent away from my family.

Ama burst into the suite and immediately started crying. A momma's boy myself, I hugged her and also started to cry. Jefe watched uncomfortably from the sidelines like a jilted lover.

In the year and a half since my uncle had taken five shots to the face, the three of us had given the border—and the cartel that controlled it—a wide berth. After Nando's death, my mother had been terrified that the Arellanos would come after me, and Jefe had not disagreed that there was cause for worry. He was afraid for me too. My father needed time to figure out if the cartel considered Nando's death payment enough to satisfy his debts. Both my parents thought I should be sent somewhere far away, for my own safety.

Since leaving the customs brokerage business after the FBI's visit, I had been a full-time student. I had gone straight into graduate school at USD after earning my BA, without even taking a pause. My parents now thought I should get away from California for a while. But the last thing I wanted during this awful period in my life was to take time off from school while I went on the lam.

At the time of Nando's death, I was just finishing up my first semester of grad school. I didn't want to quit, but I also didn't want to catch a stray bullet by staying in San Diego. I did a little research and found out that USD had a sister school in Argentina, so off I went to Buenos Aires to study for the semester.

The intended purpose of my temporary move to South America was to continue my studies while not getting killed. While most students taking a semester abroad probably aren't running from a notoriously ruthless drug cartel, I shared in the experience, common to that group, of gaining a whole new perspective that can only come by being far from home.

Although I was a twenty-six-year-old man who had run a business with more than three hundred employees, traveled the world playing polo, and seen one of my closest relatives assassinated, I was still sheltered in a lot of ways. I understood the complexities of elite and nefarious segments of society, but I had not really lived on my own.

Because my mother had never wanted her only child, her "little baby," to live far away, I had not just stayed in the state for college, I had remained in the same city! Even when I didn't live *with* my parents, I had always lived close enough to them that if I wanted to go home for the night, I could. My social circle was intertwined with theirs. The bulk of my friends had either attended my longtime school Francis W. Parker or were the children of family friends. My world included Malaysian princes, Tijuana nightclubs, yacht parties, and fast cars bought with laundered money. But it was also pretty provincial.

Now, six thousand miles from home, I was for the first time truly on my own. The distance offered me space in which to reflect—not just on myself but also on my father. As I expanded my horizons through a different social scene, city backdrop, and entire culture, I started to awaken from what seemed like a long slumber. In Argentina, I was finally waking up to the truth of who my dad was and all he had done.

Throughout my life, I'd been processing threats: from those that originated in the outside world and were about going after my family to those that were made by my father from within our family. Between one threat and another, I was always in survival mode. I'd grown up with packing bodyguards dropping me off at elementary school. I'd spent a summer during middle school on the lam. In situations like these, it doesn't come naturally to spend too much time thinking about the shit that's actually going down. Better to keep moving.

Now that I was removed from the next crisis, and from my father just breathing down my neck, I was able to feel the emotions that had been buried under stress and fear. I started to unearth a resentment against my dad that I didn't even know had been accumulating over the years. It was fucking bullshit what he had done to our family. He had known all along that his illegal activities put the lives of my mom and me in danger, I realized. Why else would he have had bodyguards protecting us?

My dad frequently railed against my mother's family: my grandfather never appreciated how he got the old man out of jail; my uncle spectacularly screwed up the land project, paying with his life; my grandmother continued to deny my mother the inheritance she was due.

But my father's memory of events only went as far back as it served him. As far as I was concerned, he was the catalyst for everything that had gone wrong. If he hadn't involved Abuelo in the Dólares Controlados scam in the first place, my grandfather wouldn't have ended up in jail. If my uncle had remained an employee of PL Exchange, he wouldn't have gone over his head in the land development project.

In those scenarios, we might not have ever become wealthy, but I didn't give two shits about money. What was left of the King of the Peso's empire anyway? Or the Gutierrez family's? Nando had attempted to run Abuelo's import-export business for a year after I left the office for good. I had known my uncle didn't have the capacity to run his father's business, but I still was shocked by the speed of its demise. The formerly amazing organization had begun a hundred years earlier with the customs patent Abuelo had inherited from his own father. Once the business no longer had anyone to care for it, though, it had fallen like a house of cards. I blamed my father for bringing my grandfather over to the wrong side of the law.

If it weren't for that motherfucker, I thought, *I would have such a different life, a better life.*

My semester abroad provided an opportunity not only to ask questions about my father but also to look for answers. When I first arrived in Buenos Aires, I didn't have any friends or distractions. For the first time in a long while, I could pause and think for a moment. So much had happened to my family so quickly. While I was in the middle of it, I hadn't really known a lot about the true story behind our change in fortune. But I was computer savvy, so I spent a lot of time on my laptop, searching newspaper and university databases to find anything written about my father, uncle, or the foreign exchange.

Out of all the references to my father that I found, one 1994 report on criminal activity in Mexico during the 1980s and 1990s in Mexico stood out: Given the countless political reforms that have been adopted in Mexico over the past 150 years, the chances of uncorrupt politicians and a safer Mexico are unlikely. Mexico's real-life Don Corleone, Pietro La Greca, just celebrated his seventieth birthday. So notorious and powerful is La Greca that Mexican newspapers openly talk about his involvement in fraud, smuggling, and money-laundering activities that he conducts with impunity.

Mexico's real-life Don Corleone?

The fact that the article compared my father to a fictional mob figure was telling. I started to see how even the articles about him reinforced the bullshit air of mystique he'd built up around himself. His persona as the godfather of Mexico was nothing more than a facade.

Sure, he was a bad man. But I also knew that threats were what my dad used to get his way, and that he actually carried out only a fraction of them. My dad the Barker, I realized, hid behind his bark. Once I understood that, his anger, which had held my mom and me captive all this time, no longer had any power over me.

I didn't discover this until the three of us were reunited in Hawaii, where I traveled after my semester in Argentina. My parents, who had gone as far east as Halifax during this period of time, felt it still wasn't safe for me to come home yet. We had settled on my going to Hawaii because we had family friends there, and they could take me in while I attended a few classes at the University of Hawaii. As soon as I arrived, Jefe and Ama came to visit for a week. My mother couldn't bear to be apart from me any longer.

In our hotel suite, with an idyllic view of the Honolulu skyline and glittering ocean as a backdrop, my father's mood grew stormy. As if he were determined to make it a real family reunion, Jefe turned on my mom and, out of nowhere, began attacking her for something so inconsequential that I no longer remember what it was. His reasons didn't matter because his playbook was always the same. Whether it was over the shade of dress my mother had picked out or me stumbling over my awkward adolescent limbs, he'd hurled insults at us in a cruel campaign to make us feel small and ashamed.

Our reactions had been consistent too. We always took the abuse and the blame. We bowed down to him as a coping mechanism. We wanted to get out from under his rule but were too scared to, so we simply obeyed.

All my life, I had feared my father and watched him degrade my mother. But not in that hotel room in Hawaii. In that moment, I saw him for what he was: a bully, a small little man, who made himself feel big by pushing around those who were weaker than he was. I wasn't weaker than him anymore, though. I was a six-foot-four twenty-six-year-old, and my dad was five foot nine and in his seventies. I could take him down in a second. Why was I still scared of his bite? That bite was a bunch of bullshit.

I lunged at my father, grabbed him by the shirt, and threw him up against the wall.

"You yell at my mother one more fucking time, I will kick your goddamn ass!"

I pushed him up against the wall again as if to punctuate my sentence. "Never fucking yell at her again! Never do it."

For the first time, I saw all the fear in the world in my dad's eyes. His son was about to kick his ass, and he couldn't do anything about it.

Then I looked over at my mom. I saw fear in her eyes, too, but of a totally different variety. She had no idea what was going to happen next. For the first time ever, her son had stood up to his dad. The alarm in her expression was clearly tinged with pride.

My dad left the room like a dog with its tail between its legs. He exited so quickly, he left without his jacket or wallet. About two hours later, he returned, and I apologized.

"Dad, I'm sorry for yelling at you and for pushing you," I said. "As a son, I should never have done that."

I was bullshitting him. I wasn't sorry. I didn't want to apologize to my father, but I did it to protect my mom, who still had to live with the bastard.

"I thought you were going to hurt me," he said.

In his downcast expression, there was nothing but fear. Although I had him by the balls, I decided I would continue to play the subservient son for as long as I needed to.

The difference was that now, I knew that when the time came, I could take him down.

It would be almost a decade later before my mom found the same courage to stand up to my dad. Unfortunately, she only lived for four more days after she did.

The summer my parents came to visit me in Hawaii, my mom was in remission after battling cancer for a second time. It had recurred in her other breast, and once again, she had chosen to do a lumpectomy over losing the breast. After another course of radiation and chemo, everything seemed to be fine.

Then, starting around 2000, she began to experience a general feeling of pain in her bones. Her doctor reassured her that it was arthritis. Eventually, my mom insisted it wasn't arthritis but something else. She turned out to be right. An MRI revealed she had cancer all throughout her bones.

By that time, I was long out of business school and firmly entrenched in corporate America, working in Carlsbad, doing sales for a financial-planning software company that was owned and operated by evangelical Christians. There at that firm, which created computer programs for meticulous organization of one's money, I thrived. I managed the largest clients at the organization, not because I knew the product better but because I knew people. I could sense their moods without them having to say a word. A lilt in the voice, pursed lips, or myriad other small, physical tells were all clues about whether a client was angry or satisfied. I'd learned that not at business school but from my dad. The only difference between a con man and a salesman is the job. If I were a criminal, I'd have used that knowledge to con someone. But I was in corporate America, so I was building relationships.

At the time I moved back home to take care of my mother, I was as far away as I possibly could be from the corruption and chaos called "business" that took place along the San Ysidro border. My by-the-book job was the one normalizing element for my family as I watched Ama slowly die over the next two and a half years. During that time, even though I was in my thirties, my mom and dad drove me to work in the morning and picked me up at the end of the day. It gave my mom pleasure during that shitty time to participate in the routine of shuttling me to and from the office, where she liked to deliver cookies and offer other little displays of maternal devotion.

I poured every inch of my soul into caring for my mom. I felt it was the least I could do for the woman who had, for so long, done the same for me. I took her to all her appointments and advocated for her with the health-care providers. The doctors were instructed to call me whenever they had any information to relay. So I was the one who took the call when her doctor called with the news that the cancer had spread to her brain.

"There's nothing we can do for your mother," he said.

I felt like a failure and continued to feel like one as her condition deteriorated despite my best efforts. I bathed her, helped her go to the bathroom and clean herself up. I spoon-fed her. One night I woke up to a noise and found her walking, naked and disoriented, throughout the house. Again, this felt like my fault. I told myself she could have hurt herself. From then on, I lay next to her in bed, holding her hand, as the cancer tormented her for most of the night.

I put so much pressure on myself, I felt like I was breaking apart. I was physically and emotionally exhausted from being my mother's sole caretaker. Watching her deteriorate in front of me was devastating. I shut out most of the outside world, but my group of friends from Francis W. Parker, whom I remain close to until this very day, found a way to support me. Beamer and his wife, Jen, would bring me lasagna every Tuesday night.

My sole focus was my mother. I had to do everything for her, including making her estate plan at a point when she was so weak, she could hardly hold the pen to sign the papers. I stood in the shower while I bathed her and watched as she winced because the water hurt her skin. I was the only one taking care of her. My mom's friends pleaded with my dad, telling him: "Picho needs help. He can't do this alone." But Jefe refused to get a nurse.

I hadn't expected any better from my dad, whom I had written off long ago. But I was deeply hurt by my grandmother, who didn't even call Ama when we found out the cancer had spread to her bones. Mother and daughter had never patched up their differences after my uncle's death. They no longer talked at all. Having decamped to her wealthy daughter-in-law's house, where she remained, Abuela was angry about all the loss she had experienced in her life. The former-beauty-queen-turned-matriarch had once run a staff of more than half a dozen domestic workers. Now, she had lost everything, including her husband, son, home, and pride.

Abuela had taken a lot of satisfaction in the fact that Don Fernando had put all the properties he bought in her name. After Abuelo died without a will—not uncommon in Mexico, where cultural machismo made one's mortality unthinkable—she owned her home in Rancho Santa Fe; two houses and a complex of twenty-two warehouses in TJ; the ranch and surrounding land in Rosarito, as well as a warehouse in the city; seventy acres in La Gloria, a region between Rosarito and TJ; and the building on the border that once housed the customs brokerage. A cash payout from the foreclosure on my grandmother's Rancho Santa Fe home—and the payment of my uncle's life—had placated the cartel. The bank had taken ownership of the Rosarito development. And Abuela had given Monique the warehouses and homes in TJ.

Jefe had pressured her hard to make the customshouse building Ama's inheritance. He started right after Nando's death and kept the pressure up for more than ten years. He knew that the property, on the busiest border in the world and steps from the US customs building, was the crown jewel of Don Fernando's eroding empire.

The building my grandfather built never stood empty. Its prime location ensured that it would always be in demand. As soon as the customs brokerage went out of business, we rented it out to other retailers, including some pharmacies that had become a big presence along the border. Many Americans were now crossing the border in order to get their medicine cheaper in Mexico. The building, in my father's eyes, was the big win.

Abuela hated my father by that point, but she was also scared of him. She and Monique still believed my dad had been instrumental in Nando's assassination. And he didn't disabuse them of the false notion that he had any power over the cartel. Instead, he stoked their fears, playing a role like he always did in order to get what he wanted. Abuela caved to my father and handed over the customshouse building and the land in La Gloria. He sold the land immediately and pocketed the money. His cut for striking the deal, I guess.

Once it was time for Abuela to physically sign over her properties to Monique and Ama, my father sent me as the proxy for my mother, who was now too weak to do much more than lie in bed. We had tried our best to keep my grandmother apprised of my mother's declining health, but our efforts had been to no avail. It seemed that Abuela was just as stubborn as my dad when it came to holding on to her grudge. But now there was no more time to waste. If she was going to make good on what she promised my father, then she would have to sign over the properties to my mother before Ama died. Whether or not Abuela realized deep down that my mother's death was imminent, nobody knows. Either way, she finally agreed to sign the papers.

I went alone to a notary in TJ to meet my grandmother and Monique. After we completed the official business, Abuela turned to me and casually asked, "How's your mother?" Her tone had all the interest and concern of a server in a restaurant asking me how my burger was. I was furious.

"Abuela, she's going to die. She's dying."

"No, she's not."

I bent down and clenched my fists and jaw. "Why can't you understand she is dying? We already told you."

She continued to repeat that I was wrong. She seemed to consciously choose not to believe me. There was no use in arguing. Maybe my grandmother, who had already lost one child and couldn't contemplate the thought of losing another, was in denial. So many lies had been told among our family members over the years that it was impossible to trust anything anyone said. In that way, I didn't blame her. Despite all the anger and heartbreak, I had to leave it alone. I'd gotten what I came for—the building Abuelo constructed on the border—and now it was time to go.

I conducted the entire errand alone. Deception ultimately breeds loneliness. That sentiment sums up my father's relationship with his friends and family, myself included. Even though he was the one who had set up the whole thing, he didn't come with me and stand by my side while I signed the papers in TJ. He sent me down there alone to face Monique and Abuela. It felt just like the times he'd sent me to hawk our stuff at the Newport Beach pawnshop alone. Or when he'd left me to hold my mother in the shower alone. Ama was the one who had always been my companion, the one who made sure I didn't feel alone. And now I was losing her.

By the time I signed the papers that made her heir to my grandfather's building, the cancer in her brain had spread to such an extent that often she didn't understand what was going on or even where she was. Ama was aware that I had gone to Mexico for the day to do something that would be hard for me but also very important for our family. Because of that, she forced my dad to go to Kentucky Fried Chicken. When I got home, she had transferred the chicken, mashed potatoes, and gravy to a plate for me. She couldn't cook anymore, but she was still determined to give her son a meal.

Despite her quickly deteriorating state, my mother retained her pride until the very end. Perhaps it was knowing that she had nothing else to lose that gave her the self-respect and strength to finally tell my father what she really thought. One day, four days after I had gone to the TJ notary, my dad started going off on me about my job.

"You need to break off from that petty little company," he said. "You need to be man enough to start your own thing."

The idea was nonsense. That office was my sanctuary. My employers had been very understanding of my situation with my mother's illness. I had been at my desk when I got the call from the doctor that the cancer had spread to her bones. Afterward, my bosses, seeing that I was upset, took me into an office and prayed with me. People at that company cared about me.

But what did my dad know about empathy and kindness? As the three of us were huddled around the kitchen island, he kept drilling at me, saying I could make much more money on my own. It was always about money with him.

Then something happened that never had before. My mom, holding herself up on the island's counter with the last of her strength, screamed, "Stop talking to him like that!"

My mom had finally had it.

"I have hated you for so long," she yelled at him. "You caused this! Because of you, we've been suffering. For years and years and years. It's all your fault. You're no good. I can't believe I defended you all those years with my father. There's nothing I want more than to divorce you."

In that moment, all the aggression toward my father she had suppressed over their thirty-six-year marriage was liberated. She did not mince any words. Despite the cancer having overtaken her brain, she had a moment of undeniable clarity, and I was standing right behind her, smiling. After years of verbal and emotional abuse that had kept her a victim, I thought, *She's letting it all out.*

My father was shocked at the vitriol pouring out of my mother. He hadn't had a clue how angry she was with him. Once he got the picture, he was an emotional wreck. He cried in the car with me twice that day.

"She hates me," my dad said. He was the picture of defeat, with his shoulders slumped and his head hung low.

"Yes, she does," I said, "and I'm not too far behind."

I don't know how she mustered such rage, considering her weakened state. But she did. That was how much she hated him.

At first, I mistook the energy and lucidity her anger had sparked as a sign that the recent downturn in her health might be only a temporary setback. I really thought there was hope, because for about a day after she lashed out at my dad, Ama was *there* again. I don't understand why this happened, but we had real conversations and moments, just like old times.

The most touching was when Trevor showed up with his new baby boy, Brooks. My mom, who had spent much of the last several months out of it from the pain or disoriented, was her old self when she saw that new infant. She returned to the nurturing den mother she had been to all my friends while we were growing up, dispensing kindness, hard truths, and good food, depending on what the situation required. In this case, she offered Trevor nothing but wholehearted praise.

"He is so beautiful," she told him as she cradled Brooks in her frail arms. "I am so proud of you."

Could she be getting better?

But no. In fact, she was just getting ready to die. Perhaps that, in the end, was what gave her the courage finally to stand up to my father. I don't know why she never left him, if she hated him so much. I suspect it was because she was too scared—either for herself or for me. There were many ways that my father could go after us.

On April 15, 2006, at the age of fifty-seven, my mother passed away.

At the end of her life, she had been in so much pain. Not long after we found out the cancer had spread to her bones, she sat at the end of her bed, defeated. Her hair had started to fall out, and she had lost a lot of weight. I knelt before her, and she reached out to touch my head.

Stroking it just like Abuelo used to, she said, "I don't want to be here anymore. It hurts too much. It's time to let me die."

Although she was telling me it was the beginning of the end, I didn't listen to her. There was no way for me to prepare for her death. When I lost my mother, I lost my faith in life and my love for people. My father was a living reminder of how unjust and cruel the world was. Why did she have to die so young, leaving me alone to deal with that asshole? As I thought about all the pain and anguish Jefe had caused Ama—who spent her short life mediating and mitigating his anger for me—I was left with only one thought.

Now I hate him too.

CHAPTER 17

The Student Becomes the Master

Michelle and I had just sold our condo and were looking for a new place to live while we rented a tiny apartment above a pizza joint. My wife was in her third trimester, and there were a lot of moving pieces as we anticipated the arrival of our first child. Busy professionals with more than twenty-five years of experience in our field, we traveled a lot for our corporate jobs, where we had built strong reputations. On our way home from a business trip to New York in the fall of 2013, we were walking through the airport in Minneapolis to make our connecting flight when I saw that Gloria, my dad's secretary, was calling. A hard-nosed Mexican woman who knew her way around the courts, Gloria managed all the operations at the customshouse building for my father.

After Ama died, Jefe had asked me for power of attorney for the customs building on the border, which my grandmother had given me control of in the proxy papers I had her sign before my mother died. At the time, I was busy with my corporate career, and he had the time to devote to keeping the building rented and in good shape. He needed the income; I didn't. Plus, the last thing I wanted was to deal with a building that was a painful reminder of the loved ones and life I had lost forever. So I agreed to his request on one condition: "Look, Dad, just promise me that you won't sell it."

"I won't," he vowed. "This is your future."

Gloria had loved my mother, and she'd promised her that if Jefe ever tried any funny business, she would let us know. Now, she was calling to tell me that I was my dad's latest mark. "Pichito, I don't know what you should do with this news," she said, "but your dad's trying to sell your building." I wasn't surprised that Jefe had betrayed me. But it was monumental that Gloria had betrayed Jefe.

The rift between my father and me that began after I returned from Argentina had only grown larger in the years after my mother's death. I had gone full-on legit. Not only did I have a rewarding job in the financial tech industry, but at this point, I had also been married for three years.

After I lost Ama to cancer, I jumped into work and dating wholeheartedly because I didn't want to be at home with my dad. Michelle was not only a smart, beautiful woman with the sunniest smile I had ever experienced; she was also a work colleague. She remembered my mom bringing cookies to the office. I proposed to her with my mother's first engagement ring, which my dad had never hawked. Ama wore it right up until the end, when her hand swelled up so badly from a chemo treatment that the ring had to be cut off. She died without it on, and Michelle and I transformed it into a ring that was a nod to my past but, at the same time, all hers.

I had changed a lot over the years. My father, on the other hand, was exactly the same. He was still living beyond his means and conning others into thinking he was someone he wasn't. That included Judy, his girlfriend half his age. She wanted a house, so my dad told her he'd buy her one. The only problem was that he didn't have the down payment. Despite all his cars and big tips, he didn't actually have any money. He burned through the $55,000 my grandfather's building brought in every month by living large. Jefe, who needed his girlfriend, had decided to sell the building so he could buy her a house. *My* building.

I hung up with Gloria, took a deep breath, and immediately told Michelle what was going on while walking through the airport. I needed to put a plan together, but I was confident I could take him down. I knew all his tricks and moves. I knew that his bark was way worse than his bite. He didn't even have a bite. Mostly, though, I knew that money was always how he wielded power. To take my father down, I had to choke all his money sources, because if he didn't have money, he couldn't bullshit people.

The tech-savvy son of an elderly immigrant, I had possession of all his passwords and IDs for all his bank accounts. All the times that I had to reset his Verizon password, and all his other passwords, finally stood to my benefit, because now I had every little bit of financial data I needed to squeeze my dad.

There was one other thing I knew about my dad, though, and that was that when it came to his money, one had to tread very carefully. I needed Michelle to be on board, and she was expecting our first child.

"Are you ready to go up against one of the most notorious men in all of Mexico?" I asked her in front of the Delta terminal. "There's only one way this goes. And it's war."

This decision needed to be *our* decision. On the plane, we nervously talked through all the possible scenarios. By the time we touched down in San Diego, Michelle, being the kick-ass wife, said she had my back and was all in with whatever I decided. Michelle was brave, but she also trusted me. It was a monumental risk I was taking, but I was the patriarch of my own family now. I had to protect my inheritance along with my wife's and child's interests, which very much included the customs building that was worth millions. I would have preferred to avoid any possibility of putting my family in jeopardy. But I believed I could beat my dad, or I would have never set out to reclaim my building. Don't get me wrong; I was scared. Michelle and I were headed into a battle with a man who would rather leave a wake of destruction than let anyone best him. To make matters worse, we were cutting off his most cherished possession—money.

Back at home, I paced miles in the little apartment above the pizza joint. Knowing how high the stakes were, I put together the pieces of my plan with extreme care. That began with finding the right lawyer. Normally I would call friends to get a referral, but I didn't want anyone other than my wife to know what I was up to. So I went online and found Frank, a lawyer who had licenses in California, New York, and Mexico. I gave him the unvarnished truth about my situation: I needed to revoke power of attorney over a very valuable piece of land from a wily man, who was also my father and who was trying to sell the property out from under me. Despite its complications, Frank took my case.

For a month, we crafted the plan that I put into motion on October 31, Halloween. It was the most nerve-racking day of my life, going up against my dad, but it also felt so good to get there. With Michelle riding shotgun the whole time, I drove to Tijuana and parked outside the building. The private investigator my lawyer had hired texted Frank and me his every move as he set out to serve Jefe the official revocation of power of attorney at his apartment complex in San Diego. (In Mexico, such a document has to be physically handed over to the person with that power, but my lawyer found that Mexican law allowed for its delivery on US soil.) The PI texted when my dad pulled into the complex and, after knocking on Jefe's door, he handed the papers to my startled father.

As soon as I saw the text saying that my father had been served, I pressed "Send" on the emails I had drafted, which informed every tenant of the new state of affairs with the building. Then I walked into the building and told those tenants who were there in person that my father's power of attorney had been revoked.

"All rents will now be coming to me," I explained. "He will not be let inside the building in any way, shape, or form."

I had hired off-duty Mexican federal police to surround the building while I made my calls. I couldn't allow my dad to pass through the door for any reason, because the minute he walked in, he could squat the property, and I would be fucked. My father knew that, which was why he hightailed it over to TJ from San Diego as soon as he got served.

By the time he arrived at the door of Abuelo's building, it was too late. The private police were stationed at the entrance. From inside, I watched my father screaming, "What the fuck is going on?" He could yell as much as he wanted; he wasn't getting in.

Germán, who had driven my father from La Jolla to TJ, approached the building. He now had a regular job at an air filtration place from 4:00 a.m. to 1:00 p.m., but by 2:00 p.m. he would be helping out my dad, running errands or driving him around to places like In-N-Out Burger, which my father loved so much at the end of his life.

I told the guards that Germán could pass, but I kept the door open so my father, within earshot, could hear what I had to say.

"Germán, he's trying to sell the property that Don Fernando built," I said. "He can go fuck himself. He's not coming in here for anything."

This was the bait. I knew the exact effect my words would have on my dad, who did not take kindly to the word *no*. He was going to fly off the handle. Jefe already had a bad temper. Getting barred from his sole source of income would be enough to make him explode.

I also knew he would be unable to resist getting in the last word. Once I shut the customshouse door, the only way for my father to reach me was by phone. If I didn't pick up, he would have to leave a message, and I was confident he would stick his foot way into his mouth. While I was in my car driving home but still in TJ, about to cross the border, I saw his number flash on my cell phone. I let the call go to voice mail. And that's when he threatened my life.

"You cross that border into Mexico," he said, "and I will put you in your tomb."

I took my father at his word, and after I went back to the US, I didn't cross the border again, not even to check on my grandfather's building. I didn't have to. I had hired enough security and people to take care of the place that I wasn't worried. The building's rental revenue, which now went into my pocket and not my dad's, more than covered the expenses.

The voice mail—which I have until this day—was proof enough for me to get a restraining order against him by an American judge. I knew Jefe didn't understand what a restraining order meant. He didn't know the first thing about US law. Did this mean he was going to jail or not? He didn't have a clue. However, if there was one thing my dad feared more than anything or anyone in Mexico, it was crossing the US government. That was because he knew that if he wound up in an American prison, he was fucked. The restraining order, however, was simply a diversion tactic. While Jefe spun his wheels about what it meant, he wasn't paying attention to the fact that I was depleting and closing down all his bank accounts (except for the sole account I wasn't a cosigner on).

My father could threaten me all he wanted, but his first line of attack—intimidation—wasn't working. My in-laws weren't taking any chances, however. They had heard about Jefe's reputation on a cruise they took shortly after I married their daughter. My mother-in-law had engaged a Mexican couple she met in the ship's Jacuzzi with conversation by asking if they had ever heard of Pietro La Greca. "My daughter married his son," she said. The couple's reaction was to exit the Jacuzzi, the husband mouthing to his wife the word *mafioso*.

After my father left his voice mail, my father-in-law—a former marine and gun enthusiast—brought over an arsenal of weapons to our two-bedroom condo.

"I'm not a gun kind of guy," I told him when I saw the stockpile.

He laughed at my admission, and to get a giggle out of an old-school, Pittsburgh-raised marine drill sergeant was no small thing.

Once my father realized I wasn't going to bow down to his bark, he decided he needed to get a lawyer or a fixer in TJ. But to get either of those, he needed money. I had completely cut off all his cash. He tried to bullshit me into believing he'd never intended to sell the building, but I had found the proof in papers he left at the office before I barred his reentry. His only lifeline came from a friend who gave him gift cards to buy groceries.

He tried to get my aunt Anna, his youngest sister still living in Italy, to give him money. She called me to verify what he was saying—that I was screwing *him* over—and when I told her the real story and played the recording, she refused to give him one cent. He eventually conned the family with whom he had been negotiating the sale of the building to front him $10,000 so he could hire a lawyer to get back power of attorney.

Jefe hired Carlos Ezquerro, one of the sleaziest lawyers in all of TJ. Ezquerro's big selling point was that he was the lawyer for the notoriously corrupt TJ police force. He had represented a ton of dirty cops, who owed him. But I had hired Mexican federal police because the customs building was on federal land, and TJ's police jurisdiction didn't extend that far.

Ezquerro wasn't getting anywhere. My dad had no case. It seemed, however, that the lawyer was going to use something other than the law to return the building to my father.

One day, while Germán was driving Ezquerro back to Mexico, the lawyer began to brag. "Man, that little kid doesn't know what's coming to him," he said, referring to me. "When he crosses that border? As soon as he comes back to Mexico, we're going to grab him and beat the fuck out of him. He's going to learn his lesson."

Germán turned around to face the lawyer. "You lay a hand on Picho, and I will kill you," he said. Germán pulled over on the freeway about a mile and a half from the border and told the man, in a tone that made it clear that he meant it when he said, "Get out of the car." Once the lawyer had exited, Germán drove off.

He called me as soon as he could to tell me what had happened. "Picho, please promise me you won't cross the border," he said. "I am not going to work for your dad anymore. I will not be in the middle of this, but if I am on any side, it's your side. Just do not cross that border."

Germán made money with my dad, but he *loved* me. When push came to shove, love came first for Germán. To this day, Germán protects me, taking pictures of the properties I own in Mexico, making sure I'm up to date, and bringing me homemade tortillas from Teresita, who is still going strong at ninety-plus years of age.

My dad was a whole other story. Even though he was running out of options, he kept doing everything he could to fight me. With his girlfriend as his new chauffeur, he drove back and forth to TJ to convince whatever cronies he had left in the Mexican press to publish disparaging stories about his own son. Before the stories could make it to print, however, my dad had his fall while exiting the SUV.

His balance hadn't been so great in the last couple of years, and he'd fallen a couple of times before. Maybe the size of the SUV tripped him up. Still loyal to Bentleys and Mercedes until the end, he wasn't used to the high ground clearance on sports utility vehicles. Whatever the reason, somehow he tore almost every single ligament in his neck and was rushed to the hospital. A tough old guy, he survived the emergency surgery and improved enough that after two weeks, he was transferred from the ICU to an off-site rehabilitation facility for continued care.

"It's unbelievable!" I told my wife. "This fucker's going to make it."

But my dad didn't make it. He contracted pneumonia at the rehab facility and on February 25, 2014, passed away.

The day he died, Michelle and I went to see him. Although I was comforted by having Michelle by my side, it was rough for me. I really didn't want to, but when I got the call that he wasn't going to make it past the next three hours, I came to say goodbye.

I took his hand and held it. That's when I noticed he was wearing my Rolex. But this was not the watch my uncle had given me and that Jefe had pawned after his bid for the sports book concession failed and he fell out of favor with Garza. This was the Submariner Jefe and Ama gave me when I was in elementary school. I had, without telling my mother, handed it over to my dad to pawn back when he was selling all our stuff.

I was surprised that he hadn't taken the Rolex to sell in Newport Beach like he had the rest of our belongings. Seeing it on his arm now, I thought about the question that had nagged me my whole life: Does he love me or not? He had brutalized my mom and me with his words, had put our lives in jeopardy, had stolen from us. He'd gone to his deathbed having tried to steal my inheritance. Still, there were times when Jefe had been, first and foremost, my dad.

One moment that stood out happened at the homecoming football game in tenth grade. The team we were playing was ranked number nine in the county. That didn't mean anything to my teammates and me. Convinced we were better than those guys, we pumped ourselves up and whooped their asses all over the field. Halfway through the fourth quarter, my pal Jason picked up a fumble and ran it into the end zone. He was celebrating his touchdown with his hands triumphantly in the air when two guys from the opposing team came up and nailed him in the back as hard as they could. Jason arched his back and fell to the ground. The rest of us went after the other team.

Instantly, the fans and family members from the other team cleared the stands to join the fight. My dad—a little guy in his made-to-measure clothes and Italian loafers, who had no interest in football—jumped up and shouted, "No way these guys go into battle on their own. Let's go!"

Leading an army of dads from my high school, he grabbed one of the stakes that held the flags in the ground, pulled it out, and charged across the field to fight with us. It reminded me of the time when I was little, when my uncle had jumped the fence to grab me before I could be gored by a bull on Abuelo's ranch. Just like Nando, my father had not hesitated in that moment to jump in to protect his son.

In Jefe's inner battle between love and greed, my mom and I had often been the casualties. Whenever he saw an opportunity, he attacked it with vigor. He was all in, always, even if the thing he'd committed to broke us as a family. He had thought that he was smarter than everyone else and would never be left on the street. In the end, however, that's pretty much how it happened, because I snatched every penny from him.

At my dad's bedside, as his life was ending, I wondered if there was a small, even unconscious part of him that was happy that his last fight had been against his son. I had only been able to stand up to my father because I knew I could take him down. That was the kind of thing that I knew would make him proud.

"You were an asshole to me," I said as I held his hand. "You could have done it a lot better, but I forgive you."

CHAPTER 18

BACK AT THE RANCH

Michelle and I decided to rent a house for a weekend trip to the Valle de Guadalupe, an up-and-coming wine region in Baja just a few miles south of Rosarito for the Thanksgiving holiday in 2016. While there, we were very close to my grandfather's property. I wondered what the ranch looked like now. I hadn't stepped foot on it since that fateful day the FBI had showed up at the customshouse building decades earlier. I put it to Michelle: "It will be weird, but do you want to see the ranch?" I wasn't sure if it was a good idea, but she was thrilled at the prospect of seeing the place where I had spent so many happy times during my childhood.

On the drive to the ranch, I couldn't help but think about how much had happened since I had last been this way. The most important of these changes was our little girl, who was now singing happily to herself in her car seat in the back seat of the car. Gabriella had been born two weeks to the day after my father's death.

I'll never forget sitting in my newborn daughter's room rocking her to sleep. I gazed down at her familiar face; Gabi is the spitting image of her grandmother Maria. Like a lot of new parents, I was overwhelmed with emotion. I counted my blessings. There was this new little infant, who made me feel as though I had a piece of my mom back on this earth. I also recognized my luck to have found a wife who cares as much for me as my mother did. I married Michelle because when she looked at me, I could tell it was one of genuine love. To this day, my wife's goal is to love me more than anyone else ever could and understand me better than I understand myself—and she has succeeded. Then there was the fact that my daughter had been born after my father passed away.

The day Jefe finally died, a huge weight lifted from my shoulders. Although he was my father, I was thankful I didn't have to deal with his lies, aggression, and mayhem anymore—and I felt even more grateful that my daughter would never have to deal with them. If I had anything to do with it, Gabi would never know the kind of chaos and fear my father had wrought. The timing was such a relief that I liked to think my mom had a hand in it. I imagined her saying in her protective way, "No, no, no. If I don't get to be a part of my granddaughter's life, you don't get to be a part of it either. You had your chance. You're done. Let's get you out of here."

"Thank you, Ama, for taking him away," I said out loud.

Michelle and Gabi were all the family I had left. Abuela had died in 2015, although it had been even longer since I'd seen her, as we didn't have a relationship before her death. I had tried to reunite with her after Gabi's birth, because she now had a great-granddaughter I thought she might like to meet. But I changed my mind when Abuela put a condition on any kind of reconciliation. "You've got to give me five thousand dollars a month going forward," she said.

Her theory was that she deserved a cut of the building in San Ysidro that she gave to my mother. The building had always been a big moneymaker. The ad revenue from the billboards that stood on it, which were seen by ninety million people annually, alone made it a gold mine.

The problem was that in my dad's last years, he had used all the building's revenue to fund his lavish lifestyle—much like Nando had done with the Rosarito project. It had taken me about two years to clean up all the debt my father had saddled the customshouse with after I took possession of it. He hadn't paid any property taxes, and he'd mismanaged the building's maintenance and rentals. Jefe could at times be masterful at whipping up money out of nowhere. But when it came to basic business skills, he was horrible, despite the fact that he thought otherwise.

When the new Mexican customs building was going up between 2013 and 2016, the government rented my entire second floor, and we punched a hole through the back of my building for easy access between my old one and their new one. To this day, the building sandwiched between Mexico and US customs, which my grandfather built in 1958, continues to provide my family a stable stream of revenue. We aren't earning high-goal polo kind of money, but we have the financial security I never had as a kid, and that's more than enough for me. Back when Abuela wanted to be paid for being my grandmother again, though, I was furious. I'd had such a confusing upbringing. I was very close to the Gutierrez side of my family until I wasn't. Because of that, I never knew who to trust or what was real. In the battle of love and greed, my family members were pulled so far apart that, in the end, we were never able to find common ground again.

While the competing narratives and composition of the teams among my family never stopped shifting, two things remained constant for me, and those were the love and loyalty of my mother and grandfather. I never doubted their devotion or the safety they provided to me. Abuelo had also been protective of many other people, his generosity reaching far beyond the scope of his family.

There are countless examples of my grandfather's kindness. One of my favorites stretches back to the years when he still used to visit the ranch. At the time, a small group of young local kids played soccer and wanted to join a league. But they came from very poor families so they didn't have the means to buy the uniforms or afford the entry fee. I was eight years old when he formed Agencia Gutierrez, vowing to the kids that he would sponsor them every year if they continued to work hard and win games.

This scrappy team from Rosarito started winning championships against bigger, more seasoned teams from TJ. Year after year, they continued to prove themselves unbeatable, and my grandfather was so proud of them. He would host them at the ranch for a day of swimming in the pool, riding around on ATVs, and feasting on carne asada. Hosting them in the exact same manner he did his most powerful friends, Abuelo didn't penny-pinch when it came to these kids, whose parents made maybe $150 a week working in factories or fields.

Once, when I was well into my forties, Germán asked me if I wanted to go to the memorial tournament in honor of my grandfather that the team, now grown men, still held every year in Rosarito. Previously unaware of this tradition, I happily went and had one of the most amazing days of my life, beginning with my arrival at the tournament. All the men were looking and pointing at me until one of them approached me, grabbed the top of my hair, rubbed it, and said, "You look exactly like him." Then he wrapped his arms around me and started to cry.

"Everyone tells me that," I said, now crying myself.

"Come with me." The man led me to his old Chevy Blazer and opened the trunk. Inside was a trove of Agencia Gutierrez memorabilia, old jerseys, championship medals, and team photos. He told me story upon story about my grandfather and expressed how much they all loved him for supporting them. Then he gave me a shirt to wear that day and asked if I would play goalie.

I stayed there until ten o'clock at night, joining with them as they ate carne asada and shared memories of my grandfather. The men were grateful for what Don Fernando had done for them forty years before.

"If your grandfather hadn't built the soccer team, I wouldn't have seen what prosperity and good fortune looked like," said one of the men, who had moved to the US and become a tax accountant in Seattle. "Your grandfather's belief in us made me who I am today."

Seeing firsthand the impact Abuelo had on so many lives only reinforced why I had always looked up to him. I missed him so much, especially in hard moments like when my grandmother demanded money in return for a relationship with her grandson and great-granddaughter. I had been trying to make things right with her and Monique and her family after all the pain my father caused and the loss of Abuelo and Nando.

But after her demand, I decided I would never have anything to do with my grandmother again.

Before Abuela died, Monique tried to reunite us. She left a voice mail on my phone saying that my grandmother was sorry and wanted to see me, but it was too late. I was hardened by then and never responded. I do regret that, to this day, I have never met my cousin, Fernando Gutierrez III. I know in him I would see the very best of my uncle.

As difficult as my family members were over their lifetimes, I still miss them. For all our misadventures, we were, in many ways, a close-knit clan. Whether we were blowing money on Bentleys and Breitlings or stabbing one another in the back, we were always deeply involved with one another.

That's part of the reason why when I pray, I pray to my family. I have a hard time asking for strength from a god, so I turn to the people who loved me. I invoke first my mother, then my grandfather. Usually I stop there, since those two spirits are with me always. But sometimes when I need a little extra oomph, I call on my uncle, Abuela, and, even on occasion, my father.

Even if you were not nice, I say in my mind, *guys, I'd love for you to jump in on this one.*

I called on the spirits of all these ancestors the day that Michelle, Gabi, and I arrived at "the ranch." Michelle was shocked by the sight of it. Whenever I had talked about the ranch, she'd envisioned wide-open spaces in the Mexican desert, flanked by mountains on one side and the majestic Pacific on the other. Now, the very same property was smack-dab in the middle of a very busy and poor city.

Over the last two decades, Rosarito had grown up around the ranch. High-rises towered above the coast from Tijuana to Rosarito and all the way down to Ensenada. When I was a little boy riding next to my grandfather to dusty peaks in the morning and trotting right into the ocean surf at sunset, there had been nothing else around. Now there was a ten-story building immediately to the right of the original ranch gate, which still remained.

The rusted gate was the entryway to a trip back in time. I swung it open and drove down the road that used to proudly display my grand-father's lovingly cared for antique cars and carriages. Right in the middle of the city, this piece of land remained, having been abandoned to time and progress.

After my uncle's death, the land he had mortgaged and remort-gaged as part of the failed property development deal was taken over by the banks. But although the bank foreclosed on the property, they didn't dare touch it, because the Arellano brothers had a second, off-the-books loan on it. And so there it sits until this day: untouched. Though the loan was not legally recorded anywhere, the bank officials were more than aware of who owned what—and they weren't about to take their lives in their hands by selling something that would piss off the TJ Cartel.

Meanwhile, the cartel didn't own the land either. As a result, the land was locked up in a financial catch-22. What the situation needed was a middleman to negotiate a deal that everyone could live with. Ironically, my dad would have been the perfect fixer for the situation if it hadn't held so much bad history for him.

The skeleton of Plaza San Fernando still remained, the concrete foundation and steel frame untouched since the day the workers left the site, never to return. The city had taken possession of the stables, which they'd knocked down, to create a municipal parking lot where they hosted sad circuses and other two-bit events.

My wife, daughter, and I walked down to the little chapel where I was once baptized. Although it was in ruins, Michelle marveled at the solemn beauty the building still retained. The white concrete walls and nave, though dirty with time, still had the peaceful air of a holy place.

Then we made our way to the ranch house, which hadn't withstood the elements as well. It was completely run-down, so that all that remained were the bones of the original estate. I was haunted by the sight of my family home, once so full of life, abandoned to decay. Hearing voices, we walked around the other side of the ruined building and found transients smoking and drinking in the empty and cracked pool.

"We've got to get out of here," Michelle said. "This has got to break your heart."

"Yeah. It's breaking my heart."

It's ironic to me that the land my grandfather, a pillar of society, worked hard to acquire is now a crumbling ghost town. He had hoped to leave a prosperous legacy for his family and community. Now, the rusted gate leads only to a shell of a house and a cracked, empty pool.

My father, on the other hand, had been a terrible businessman who was only interested in a venture as far as it benefited him. He would have been the first to admit this fact. And yet he, and not my grandfather, was the one who permanently changed the world's busiest border after an idea popped into his head, pointing to a way he could profit off other people's misfortune.

The first time I exchanged pesos for dollars in San Ysidro after my dad died, I went up to the teller and handed him my ID. I had just collected all the rents from the customshouse building, which was more than the $9,999 limit that still kicked off the tax penalty, so I had to present identification. The teller looked at my driver's license and then up at me. "This name is a very famous name here in this area," he said.

"I know. I know."

"Is he a relation?"

"Yeah, he was my dad."

When Jefe folded the PL Exchange after my grandfather's arrest, Rocky De La Fuente quickly followed suit with his exchanges. The golden era of the great peso rush had come to an end. By then, Mexicans had become inured to the swings of their currency. Running a foreign exchange was never going to be a monumental business again. But although foreign exchange no longer brought in big money, it was still a business. My dad's exit, and Rocky's, paved the way for many other operators to open up their own small exchanges. It was kind of like the breakup of the Soviet Union. Once the larger state broke up, lots of littler players got a piece.

There's no need anymore for big foreign exchanges, with a phalanx of tellers at the ready to make thousands of transactions, using millions of dollars piled up in a safe behind them—all while a mastermind sees to the comfort and entertainment of the VIPs waiting for their money. Nonetheless, people still need to change their money. They still need to send money back and forth between the US and Mexico. There is plenty of activity across the border every day, and it all takes money.

Today, the streets of San Ysidro are littered with foreign-exchange kiosks. A typical mini-mall in the area will have a check-cashing and foreign-exchange place right next to each other, alongside a 7-Eleven. Foreign exchanges are so common now, they can be found within the countless pharmacies Americans cross the border to frequent, in order to obtain cheaper meds.

Many different people need to exchange money at the border, including me. Every time I enter into one of the thousands of microexchanges all over San Ysidro, I'm reminded of the impact my dad had on the border, something that the teller exchanging my rent money made explicit when he said, "Pietro La Greca did a lot for this area."

Then he stacked my dollars neatly and got ready to hand them over. But before he did, he added, "My God, though, he was one crazy son of a bitch."

ACKNOWLEDGMENTS

Over my seventeen years in software sales, whenever the circumstance dictated the need for an entertaining tale—usually over drinks after dinner—I enjoyed sharing my family's story. After I finished, the client or colleague more often than not said, "You should write the book." I always thanked my audience for the compliment, but I never imagined my story could actually become a book. No matter how much my wife, Michelle, disagreed with me.

An unexpectedly amazing chain of events led me to this moment of pride and excitement to tell my story to the world. It all began in 2017 at a friend's pool party, where I met John Rogers. Just as I had done countless times in corporate America, I regaled John, who, unbeknownst to me at the time, is a successful Hollywood producer. Sometimes you need someone outside your circle of family and friends to support you, and John did so without hesitation. Thank you, John, for bringing your invaluable experience and unwavering commitment to this project.

By happenstance, John's brother Matt was in New York City attending an art exhibit, where he shared a drink and the details of our project with Leopoldo Gout, an accomplished visual artist, filmmaker, and writer who hails from Mexico City. John and I met with Leo one week later, and the project had a third member, who put together a professionally accomplished and successful team instrumental in bringing my story to life. Your knowledge has been a guiding light. *Muchas gracias, hermano!*

A vital member of that team is Lisa Gallagher, my publishing agent. Lisa, the foundation of this book, gracefully put the pieces in place to make this process as seamless as possible. Thank you, Lisa, for being such a skillful, hardworking professional and the rock this project needed.

Tasked with finding a writer for my story, Lisa introduced me to Rebecca Paley, who perfectly captured my voice and masterfully wrote this book. I want to thank you from the bottom of my heart. I had an amazing time getting to know you and enjoyed every minute of every one of our conversations. It has been a joy working together, and I can't wait to sip margaritas together with our families on a beach in Baja.

Thank you, Little A, for supporting this project. I want to recognize my editors, Carmen Johnson and Shari MacDonald, for their guidance and encouragement throughout the project. It has been my pleasure working with two consummate professionals. Also, a quick thank-you to Andrea Gallo for her transcription services and words of encouragement.

Two unsung heroes in my life whom I want to thank are my in-laws, Leslie and Dave Worden. You raised a wonderfully perfect daughter, and I thank you from the bottom of my heart for your committed love of and support for our family. When push comes to shove, I couldn't choose two better people to have in my corner. I sincerely love and admire you both.

This book was possible because I enjoyed, suffered, and survived a real-life family drama riddled with greed, fun, deception, death, fear, and love. My friends and family molded me into the man I am today. I am grateful to each and every one who stood by my side through the good times and, more importantly, the bad times.

With all the anguish and delight my family has caused, I have to thank all of them—Uncle Fer, Abuela, Abuelo, and even you, Jefe—for every life-learning experience I endured and sometimes enjoyed.

Thanks, Mom . . . I think about you every day and miss you so fucking much. I really wish you could have met my wife and your granddaughter. You would be so proud. If you're reading this, "You got baby."

My sweet Gabi, I love you so much. Ever since I took your little hand in mine, I have only wanted you to be proud that I'm your dad. You are my pride and joy, and every day that I watch you flourish more and more, I think of how you inspire me to be a better person. I will always protect and love you in this world and the next. Thank you for bringing me more joy than I could ever have imagined possible. Remember to go for it and stay focused on your dream to build Gabi's world.

Lastly, I want to thank my wife, Michelle, for her unwavering love and commitment to our marriage and family. The best feeling is knowing that you're my wife and you have my back. I tend to take the spotlight away from you when you deserve it, and sometimes you feel forgotten in the wake of my big personality. But I want to remind you that my spotlight is always shining on you. Thanks for being the best wife a man could dream of, raising our daughter, and making my every day worth living. I love you, Nubbles!

ABOUT THE AUTHOR

Photo © 2018 John Schnack Photography

Pietro La Greca Jr. served as a senior executive in the financial software services industry for over nineteen years. A veteran of the wealth and financial technology industry, he earned his BA and MBA from the University of San Diego. He lives in La Jolla, California, with his wife, Michelle, and six-year-old daughter, Gabi. When he isn't entertaining clients with salty stories of his colorful family's criminal past, Pietro volunteers for local charities throughout San Diego and serves on the board of trustees at an independent school in La Jolla.

Rebecca Paley is the #1 *New York Times* bestselling coauthor of multiple books and lives in Brooklyn with her family.